~ *Purchased*
with interest income
from the
library's trust fund ~

The Freshwater Angler™

FISHING WITH
Artificial Lures

CREATIVE
PUBLISHING
international

MINNETONKA, MINNESOTA

President / CEO: David D. Murphy
Vice President / Editorial: Patricia K. Jacobsen
Vice President / Retail Sales & Marketing: Richard M. Miller

FISHING WITH ARTIFICIAL LURES
By Creative Publishing international, Inc.

Executive Editor, Outdoor Products Group: Don Oster
Editorial Director: David R. Maas
Senior Editor, Project Leader: David L. Tieszen
Editor: Jeff Simpson
Technical Advisor: Mike Hehner
Managing Editors: Jill Anderson, Denise Bornhausen
Copy Editors: Janice Cauley, Lee Engfer
Creative Director: Bradley Springer
Senior Art Director: David W. Schelitzche
Mac Designer: Joe Fahey
Photo Researcher: Angie Hartwell
Studio Manager: Marcia Chambers
Studio Services Coordinator: Carol Osterhus
Photographers: Kris Boom, Buck Holzemer, Jon Liebendorfer, Bill Lindner, Jerry Robb
Photo Assistant: Tony Vavricka
Director, Production Services: Kim Gerber
Production Staff: Curt Ellering, Laura Hokkanen, Kay Swanson
Contributing Photographers: James C. Hodges Jr., Mitch Kezar, John Schneider, Doug Stamm, David L. Tieszen
Contributing Manufacturers: Abu Garcia; Berkley; Blue Fox Tackle Company; Eppinger Mfg. Company; Hart Tackle Company, Inc.; Kalin Company; Lindy-Little Joe, Inc.; Luhr-Jensen & Sons, Inc.; Lunker City; M/G Tackle, Inc - Brad and JayDee Mahs; Mann's Bait Company - Suzanne Newsom; Normark Corporation - Craig Weber; Northland Fishing Tackle - John Peterson; Outdoor Technologies Group, Ltd. - Gary King, Linda Rubis; Plano Molding Company - Jesse Simpkins; Poe's Lures/Yakima Bait Company; PRADCO - Frank Wilhelm, Jr.; Sage Manufacturing Corporation – Marc Bale, Don Green, David T. Low, Jr.; Storm Manufacturing Company - Sharon Andrews; Suick Lure Manufacturers - Steve Suick; 3M/Scientific Anglers - Jim Kenyon; Uncle Josh Bait Company
Printing: R. R. Donnelley & Sons Co.
10 9 8 7 6 5 4 3 2 1

Library of Congress Cataloging-in-Publication Data

Fishing with artificial lures : the complete guide to catching fish on spinners, plugs, soft plastics, jigs, spoons and flies.
     p. cm. -- (The freshwater angler)
     ISBN 0-86573-110-1 (hc.)
     1. Lure fishing. 2. Fishing lures. I. Creative Publishing
International. II. Hunting & fishing library. Freshwater angler.

SH455.8 .F57 1999
799.1'2--dc21

                   99-044755

Contents

Introduction

Generations of fishermen have been challenged by the idea of outsmarting fish with an artificial lure. And nearly everyone who has tossed a lure into the water has fashioned, at least mentally, an improved artificial lure that no fish could resist.

The result of this combined brainpower has been a staggering proliferation of lures in every imaginable shape, size, color and texture. But just when we conclude that it would be impossible to invent anything new, someone designs a lure that outperforms anything currently on the market.

Today's fishermen can choose from a wider selection of lures than ever before. But many anglers fail to take advantage of modern lure technology. Instead, they fish with live bait or use only a few lures that have produced for them in the past.

Even the most accomplished artificial lure fisherman would agree that there are times when live bait is more effective. But artificial lures offer several major advantages over live bait:

• They enable you to cover more water. In most instances, live bait must be retrieved slowly, limiting the area you can cover effectively.

• When the fish are biting, you can catch them more quickly. With live bait, a great deal of time is lost in rigging.

• You can go fishing without first stopping at the bait shop, and you do not face the problem of keeping bait alive.

• Live bait is illegal in some areas, so artificial lures are the only choice.

The purpose of this book is to acquaint you with each major class of lures, show you which lures work best in which situations and demonstrate the best techniques for using these lures. And we will show you dozens of little-known tricks that will make your lures more effective.

One chapter is devoted to each of the following lure classes: spinner-type lures, plugs, soft plastics, jigs and jigging lures, spoons and flies. Each chapter contains detailed information on every category of lures in that class. The plug chapter, for example, has sections on nine different categories of plugs, including four types of surface plugs and five types of subsurface plugs.

This book will also help you select the proper equipment for use with each type of lure. Without the right equipment, it would be difficult to present your lures effectively. Selecting the wrong rod and reel, for example, may hinder your casting distance or prevent you from feeling the lure working. Line that is too heavy will reduce casting distance, dampen the action of your lure and possibly spook the fish. Even minor items like snaps or swivels affect your lure's action, so it is important to use the right ones. You will also learn the best knots for use with artificial lures.

This book is sure to expand your knowledge of artificial lures and generate some fresh ideas that will help you catch more fish.

Equipment

Rods & Reels

Whether or not you catch fish on an artificial lure often depends as much on the equipment used to present it as on the lure itself. And none of your equipment is more important than your rod and reel.

Without the right rod, you may not cast far enough or accurately enough, and you may have difficulty feeling the lure's action and detecting strikes.

Manufacturers generally rate rods according to the weights of the lures they are designed to cast and the line size that can be used. Always check the specifications to make sure the rod suits the lure you will be using. Many fishermen carry several rods so they are prepared to fish lures of different weights.

Even with lures of the same weight, you may need more than one rod for different methods of fishing and kinds of fish. For example, you could use a one-ounce lure when trolling for salmon with downriggers and when casting for muskies. But downrigger trolling requires a long, limber rod, while muskie casting demands a much shorter, stiffer rod. The long, limber rod is necessary for bending into the set position and for fighting large, powerful fish on relatively light line. The shorter, stiffer rod is needed to cast the heavy lures and to set the hooks in a muskie's bony mouth.

Another consideration in choosing a rod is its length. A long rod generates more tip speed than a short one, so it can cast the same lure a greater distance. A short rod casts with a flatter trajectory, so it works better for placing your lure under a dock or an overhanging tree limb.

Action is also important. A fast-action rod has a stiff butt and midsection, bending most near the tip. This type of rod is best suited for distance casting because it propels the lure rapidly. A fast-action rod is also best for a solid hook set.

A slow-action rod bends over its entire length. It is the best choice for accurate casting because it bends more slowly, giving you more time to aim. And because the lure travels through the air more slowly, you can easily stop it on a precise target. A slow rod is also a better shock absorber, so a strong fish would have more difficulty breaking the line.

Improved rod-building technology has resulted in fishing rods that are lighter, stiffer and more sensitive than the rods of years past. Graphite rods excel for detecting subtle strikes. They telegraph a lure's wiggle or the beat of a spinner blade better than fiberglass rods. They also help you feel the lure ticking bottom or brushing the weedtops.

The reel you select, whether spinning, baitcasting or fly, must balance with your rod. The sure way to test your outfit's balance is to try casting with it. If the rod feels tip-heavy, the reel is too light. If it feels butt-heavy, the reel weighs too much.

When selecting a spinning reel, make sure that the diameter of the spool suits the line you will be using. The heavier the line, the larger the spool diameter you will need. If you attempt to wind heavy mono on a small-diameter spool, the line will come off in tight, springy coils. As a general rule, use a spool with a front flange at least 1½ inches in diameter for

6-pound mono; 1⅞ inches for 10-pound mono; and 2¼ inches for 14-pound mono.

Spinning and baitcasting reels come with a variety of gear ratios. The gear ratio is the number of times the spool revolves with each turn of the reel handle. On a reel with a gear ratio of 5:1, the spool turns five times while the reel handle turns once.

Reels with large-diameter spools and high gear ratios are needed for retrieving fast-moving lures or large quantities of line. A small-diameter spool and low gear ratio give you more power for reeling in strong fish.

Baitcasting reels should be resistant to backlashing. Backlash-prevention devices like centrifugal or magnetic brakes will keep the problem to a minimum. Reels with narrow spools work best for casting light lures, but few baitcasting reels can cast lures weighing under ³⁄₁₆ ounce.

Most fly fishermen prefer single-action fly reels because they are light, simple and trouble-free. The term single-action means that the spool revolves once with each turn of the reel handle. Multiplying reels have a gear mechanism that boosts the retrieve ratio, an advantage when handling a lot of line or trying to catch up with a fish running toward you. Automatic reels have a spring mechanism for taking up line, but they are heavier, less dependable and have less capacity for line and backing than other types of fly reels.

Lines

One of the most common mistakes when fishing with artificial lures is using line that is too heavy. Always select the lightest line suitable to the conditions. In spinning and baitcasting, heavy line reduces casting distance, is more visible to fish and may restrict the action of your lure. In fly fishing, heavy line makes a splash and may spook fish.

Fishermen who use spinning or baitcasting tackle use either nylon monofilament or braided lines. Both lines cast equally well, but monofilament is less visible in water.

In most fishing situations, use the monofilament that has the smallest diameter for its strength. Most manufacturers list the diameter on the package. Small-diameter line casts better and is less visible than larger-diameter line of the same strength.

When fishing with monofilament around objects that could cause fraying, such as weeds or other

FISHING LINES include:
(1) nylon monofilament, used primarily in light to medium applications; (2) Dacron, which has good knot strength and little stretch, and (3) braided superlines, used when a thin diameter and no stretch are important.

How to Spool On Line

LOAD fishing line onto a spinning reel by taking it off the side of the spool. If the reel turns in a counterclockwise direction, the line must come off the spool in a counterclockwise direction. This method of loading minimizes the twist in your line.

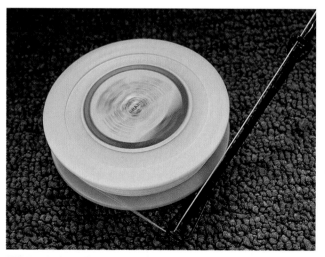

FILL a baitcasting reel with line by threading your line through the guides, then letting the spool turn on carpet while reeling. Or simply reel while the spool turns on a pencil. A baitcasting reel will not twist your line in the loading process.

obstructions, use an abrasion-resistant line. However, these lines usually have a relatively large diameter for strength and they tend to spring off the spool because of their stiffness.

Monofilament is not the best choice for setting the hook in large, hard-mouthed fish like muskies and northern pike. A low-stretch line such as Dacron® or a braided superline works better because line stretch will not dampen your pulling power.

Trollers often use special-purpose lines to reach greater depths or to indicate the depth at which their lure is running. Superlines are used to troll plugs. The line is strong, sensitive and thin, allowing plugs to go deeper. Wire line, either single- or multi-strand, is popular for deep trolling, but it can develop kinks that greatly reduce its strength. Lead-core line will not run quite as deep, but it is less prone to kinking. Metered line is color-coded, usually with a different color every 10 yards. When you hook a fish, observe the color on your spool, then let your line back out to that color when you resume fishing.

When choosing a fly line, you must match the line to your rod and to your fly. Although level (L) lines are most economical, double-taper (DT) lines can be cast more delicately and weight-forward (WF) lines can be cast farther.

Double-taper lines have a long, level section in the middle and an identical taper at each end. They roll over smoothly on the cast and land gently on the water. When one end wears out, you can reverse the line and use the other end. Double-taper lines are popular for dry-fly fishing, where long casts are seldom desirable.

Weight-forward lines have a short front taper, a thick level section, or *belly*, and a long, thin *running line* at the rear. Weight-forward lines are designed for distance casting but also work well at short range. A special kind of weight-forward line, called a *bass taper,* has a shorter, thicker belly and shorter front taper. Because a bass taper turns over with more power, it works well for casting bugs (p. 122) and other wind-resistant flies.

For even more distance, use a shooting taper (ST) line. The fly line is spliced to a separate monofilament or coated-Dacron running line. An experienced fly fisherman can easily cast a shooting taper over 100 feet.

When fishing on or near the surface, use a floating (F) line. For deeper water, you will need a sink-tip (F/S) or sinking (S) line. Most sink-tip lines have a 10-foot sinking section at the front. The rest of the line floats. Sinking lines enable you to fish deepest because the entire line sinks. But they are difficult to control in current and to lift from the water when you wish to cast.

Always wind backing on before spooling on your fly line. Most fishermen use 20- to 30-pound braided Dacron. Backing will help insure that big fish do not run out all your line. It also prevents your fly line from forming tight coils, as it would if wound directly on the arbor. Having the spool full will also provide a faster retrieve rate, important when trying to gain line on a running fish.

Tips on Caring for Your Line

RUB silicone fly-line dressing on the front few feet of a braided Dacron line. The fraying from constant casting is reduced, so you do not have to trim back line as often.

CLEAN fly line with mild soap and water to remove dirt. Then treat it with a protectant to maintain the plastic coating and help the line shoot smoothly through the rod guides.

AVOID leaving monofilament or fly lines in direct sunlight. Prolonged exposure to heat and ultraviolet rays weakens monofilament and cracks the finish on fly lines.

11

Knots for Use with Artificial Lures

Y ou can improve your success with artificials by learning the best knots for tying on lures, attaching leaders and splicing various types of lines.

Knots cinched directly to the eye are not the best choice for attaching all lures. With wobbling lures, for example, a knot tightened on the eye may restrict the side-to-side action. A loop knot, such as the Duncan loop, is a better choice in this situation. A knot cinched to the eye may cause a dry fly to become cocked on the leader, making it float unnaturally. A knot that will not allow the fly to swing, like a dry-fly clinch, prevents this problem.

When using a wire leader, you can keep its visibility to a minimum by attaching the lure with a haywire twist or a twist-melt connection.

For splicing monofilament, most anglers prefer the blood knot. But a blood knot is not the best choice for joining lines and leaders of much different thicknesses or different materials. The triple surgeon's knot, Albright special, nail knot and superglue splice are better choices.

How to Attach a Lure with a Trilene Knot

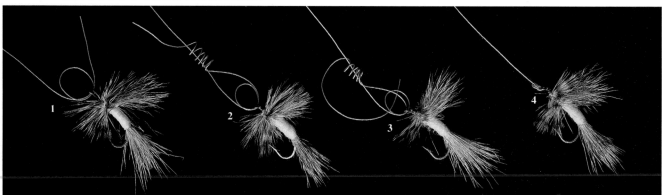

PASS the line through the eye of the hook twice from the same side, leaving a (1) double loop next to the eye. (2) Wrap the free end around the standing line about five times. (3) Push the free end of the line through the double loop. (4) Moisten the line and snug up the knot with a steady pull on the tag line and hook; trim. The Trilene knot is an excellent knot because it ties easily, stacks smoothly and has no sharp bends. It is also one of the strongest knots, with a rating of 90 percent of line strength.

How to Attach a Lure with a Loop Knot

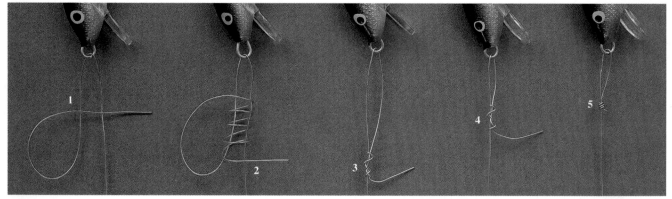

DUNCAN LOOP. (1) Pass the mono through the eye of the lure, then bend it back toward the eye to form a closed loop. (2) Holding the loop and standing line between your thumb and forefinger, wrap the end of the line around the standing line and through the loop four to six times. (3) Start to tighten the knot by holding the lure while pulling alternately on the standing line and tag end. (4) Slide the knot to the desired position by pulling on the standing line. (5) Cinch the knot in place by pulling hard on the tag end with pliers; trim.

How to Attach a Mono Leader to Braided Dacron or Monofilament Line

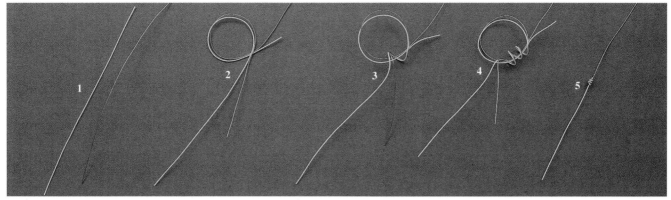

TRIPLE SURGEON'S KNOT. Splice two lengths of monofilament by (1) laying the ends alongside each other so they overlap about four inches. (2) Form a closed loop in the doubled portion of the line. (3) Pass the doubled portion that includes the free end through the loop to form an overhand knot. (4) Pass the doubled portion through the loop two more times. (5) Be sure to moisten the knot, then pull on all four lines to snug it up; trim.

How to Attach Monofilament to Wire or Heavier Mono

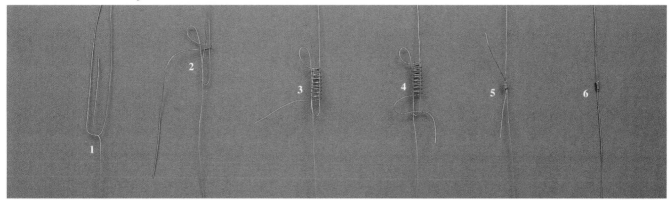

ALBRIGHT SPECIAL. (1) Double the end of a wire or heavy monofilament leader, then pass the standing line through the loop. (2) Hold the standing line against the wire or heavy mono, then wrap the free end around the standing line and leader. (3) Continue wrapping until you complete at least eight wraps, progressing toward the loop. (4) Pass the free end back through the loop. (5) Tighten the knot by alternately pulling on the free end, then on the standing line. (6) Break off the excess wire as you would with a haywire twist (p. 14); trim mono.

How to Attach Fly Line to Leader or Backing

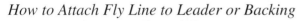
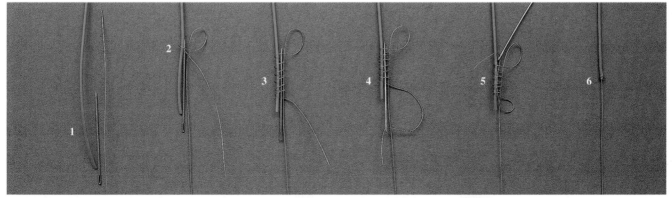

NAIL KNOT. (1) Position a needle alongside the end of the fly line and the butt of the leader. At least 6 inches of the leader butt should extend past the needle. (2) Begin wrapping the butt of the leader around the fly line, needle and standing portion of the leader. (3) Continue wrapping until you complete about five loops. (4) Insert the butt of the leader through the eye of the needle. (5) Holding the loops securely, carefully pull the needle through. (6) Pull on the butt and standing part of the leader to tighten the knot; trim fly line and mono.

How to Make a Dropper

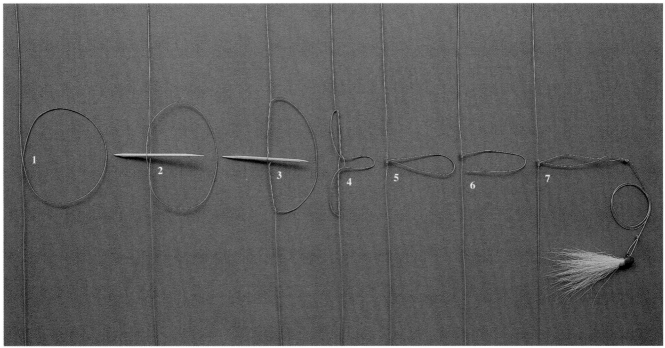

DROPPER LOOP. (1) Make a dropper for attaching an extra lure by first forming a 3-inch loop in the line. (2) Hold the doubled portion of the loop with both hands, then insert a toothpick between the lines. (3) Twist it about four times. (4) Remove the toothpick, then push the loop through the opening where the toothpick was. (5) Tighten the knot by pulling the line on both sides of it. (6) Cut one side of the dropper loop just below the knot to make a single-line dropper, or (7) attach a leader using a loop-to-loop connection.

How to Attach a Lure to Wire Line

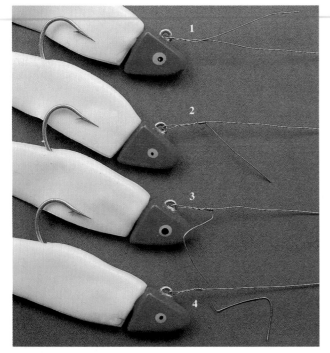

HAYWIRE TWIST. Attach your lure to a single-strand wire leader by (1) forming about three loose twists. Then (2) make about five tight wraps. (3) Bend the free end into the shape of a handle. (4) Crank the handle several times until the wire breaks off.

TWIST MELT. Attach nylon-coated leader wire by (1) passing it through the eye, then wrapping it around the end of the standing portion five times. (2) Move a lighter back and forth below the twists until the nylon melts together. If you heat it too much, it becomes brittle.

How to Snell On an Attractor

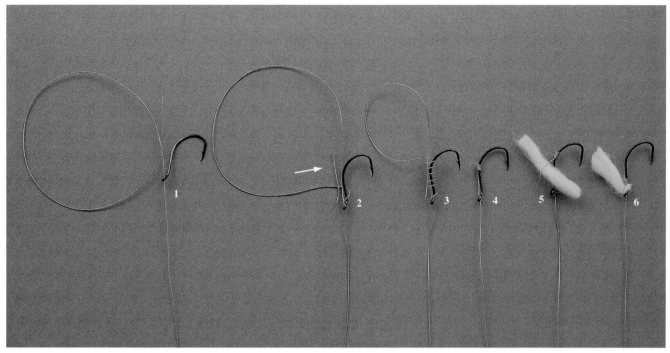

SNELL. Attach yarn or another attractor to your hook by (1) passing about 8 inches of line through the eye and making a loop above the shank. (2) Holding the hook and the loop with one hand, begin wrapping the leg of the loop nearest the eye around the hook, standing line and free end (arrow). (3) Make about five wraps, holding the turns in place with one hand while progressing toward the bend of the hook. (4) Tighten the knot by pulling first the standing line, then the free end; trim. (5) Open the loop; insert yarn. (6) Slide the snell back to the eye.

Other Knots and Connections

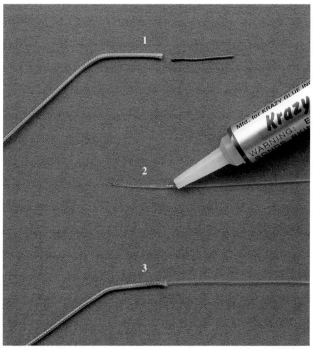

DRY-FLY CLINCH. Attach a fly by (1) passing the end of your leader through the eye, then wrapping it around the shank and back out the eye. (2) Wrap the end around the standing line five times. (3) Pass the end between the lines ahead of the fly. (4) Snug up the knot; trim.

SUPERGLUE SPLICE. Attach lead-core line to monofilament by (1) bending the line back and forth until a 1/2-inch piece of the lead breaks off. (2) Apply superglue to the mono. (3) Quickly push the mono into the nylon shell from which the lead was removed.

Leaders, Swivels & Connectors

A leader, swivel or connector that inhibits your lure's action or appears unnatural to the fish will greatly reduce the number of strikes you get.

When fishing with monofilament, you can usually attach your lure directly to the line. Most other line is too stiff or too visible for direct attachment, so you will need a mono leader. Always use the lightest leader suitable for the type of fish and the conditions. You need a heavier leader for fishing in timber or brush, for instance, than you do when fishing over a clean bottom.

Some fishermen attach their lures with heavy wire leaders regardless of what kind of fish they expect to catch. But wire leaders are unnecessary and undesirable for most types of freshwater fish.

Fly fishermen should use tapered monofilament leaders. With most flies, a level leader does not have enough momentum to unroll completely on the cast. Tapered leaders may be either knotted or knotless. Knotted leaders consist of several sections of monofilament, decreasing in diameter from butt to tip. Some fishermen tailor their own to suit the conditions. Knotless leaders are more expensive, but have no knots to pick up algae. The weight or diameter of the tippet, the front section of the leader,

depends mainly on the size of the fly you are casting. On most spools of tippet material, the weight is designated not only by the breaking strength, in pounds, but also by an X-number. As a general rule, divide the fly size by three to determine which tippet weight to use. For example, a size 18 fly would require a 6X tippet.

Most artificial lures do not require a swivel. A swivel makes the lure appear larger, may change its balance and action and could increase the chances of tangling on the cast. Without a swivel, however, many lures would twist your line. High-quality, ball-bearing swivels generally reduce line twist more than cheap brass swivels.

Some types of artificial lures, such as spoons and vibrating blades, work better when attached with a snap or split-ring. Tying your line directly to these lures decreases the amount of action and may cut your line.

A round-nosed snap is a better choice than a V-nosed snap because it allows the lure to swing more freely. Snaps made from a length of continuous wire are generally stronger than the safety-pin type. Select the smallest snap, split-ring or swivel suitable for the situation.

Tips on Using Leaders, Swivels and Connectors

MAKE a 6-inch leader from 20-pound wire line rather than using a commercial wire leader. Attach a swivel and clip with haywire twists (p. 14).

SPLICE in a keel swivel 1 to 2 feet ahead of a lure that could severely twist your line. Keel swivels work especially well for trolling.

SOLDER a split-ring to greatly increase its strength. Soldering also reduces the chances of the line slipping into the groove and fraying.

USE a wire leader only when fishing for northern pike, pickerel or muskies. No other freshwater gamefish have teeth sharp enough to cut through nylon monofilament. Many experts prefer single-strand wire to multi-strand wire because it is smaller in diameter for its strength and easier to straighten should it become curled.

Common Mistakes in Attaching Lures

ATTACHING a surface lure with heavy hardware causes the nose to sink. When you twitch the lure, it will not sputter, pop or gurgle.

USING a snap-swivel when only a snap is needed may diminish a lure's action. Buy plain snaps or use only the snap from a snap-swivel.

TYING the line in the groove of a split-ring rather than on the double wire weakens the connection. And the ring's sharp ends may fray your line.

Spinner-Type Lures

Spinner-Type Lures

Two aspects of spinner-type lures attribute to their success in both clear and murky water. In clear water, gamefish can spot the flash of the revolving blade from a distance. In murky water, they use their lateral-line sense to pinpoint the vibration from the turning blade.

Another reason for the success of these lures is the relative ease of using them. They will produce fish with a simple straight retrieve. And, when a fish strikes a spinner, it often hooks itself.

Spinner-type lures come in four basic designs. Standard spinners have a blade that rotates around a straight wire shaft. Most standard spinners have some type of weight behind the blade to make the lure heavy enough to cast. Weight-forward spinners resemble standard spinners, but the weight is ahead of the blade. Spinnerbaits have a shaft similar to an open safety pin. They have a lead head on the lower arm and a spinner blade on the upper arm. Buzzbaits resemble either standard spinners or spinnerbaits, but have a specially designed propeller.

Spinner-type lures will catch almost any kind of freshwater gamefish. These lures will work at any time of year, but they are especially effective when extremely cold or warm water makes fish lethargic and reluctant to chase anything moving too fast.

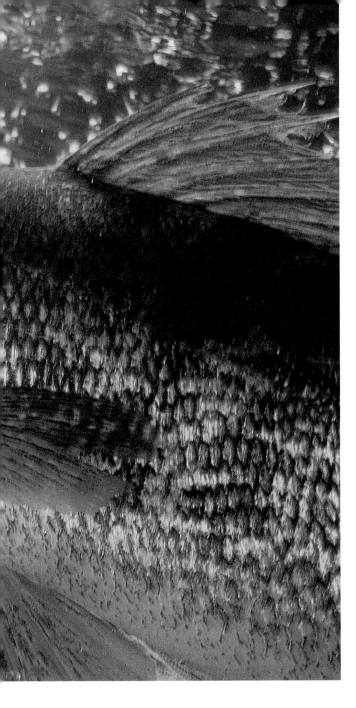

or buzzbait, use a stiff rod to drive the thick hooks into a fish's jaws.

When fishing spinner-type lures for panfish or trout, use 2- to 6-pound mono; for walleyes or small-mouths in open water, 6- to 10-pound mono; for bass in heavy cover, 12- to 25-pound mono; for casting muskie bucktails, 30- to 50-pound braided Dacron.

POPULAR BLADES include: (1) Colorado; (2) Indiana; (3) French; (4) willow leaf; (5) sonic blade, which spins at a high speed; and (6) buzzblade, which sputters when retrieved on the surface.

Most spinner blades will turn even at very slow retrieve speeds.

Different blades have different amounts of water resistance. A broad blade rotates at a greater angle to the shaft and thus has more resistance than a narrow one. A large blade has more resistance than a small one of the same shape.

The greater the resistance, the shallower the lure will run at a given speed. Generally, wide blades are best suited for slow retrieves and light current; narrow ones for fast retrieves and swift current.

Sensitive tackle will help you feel the beat of the spinner blade. If the beat stops, you may be retrieving too slowly, weeds may have fouled the lure or a fish may have struck it. When fishing a spinnerbait

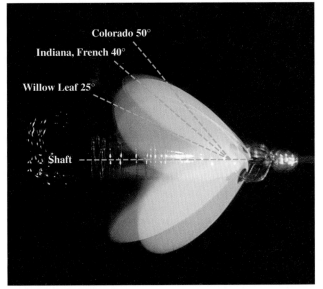

ANGLE OF ROTATION varies with different styles of blades. Colorado-style blades (above) turn at an angle to the shaft of approximately 50 degrees; Indiana and French blades, about 40 degrees; and willow-leaf blades, about 25 degrees.

Standard Spinners

The standard spinner has gained a worldwide reputation as a top fishing lure. Its simple design has remained basically unchanged for decades.

Because standard spinners sink slowly, they are most effective at shallow or medium depths. They work best in open water, but can also be fished in sparse weeds or over weedtops. They are not as weed-resistant as safety-pin spinners.

Standard spinners come in two main styles. The most common has a blade attached to the shaft with a *clevis*. It produces a strong beat easily detectable by the fish and the fisherman.

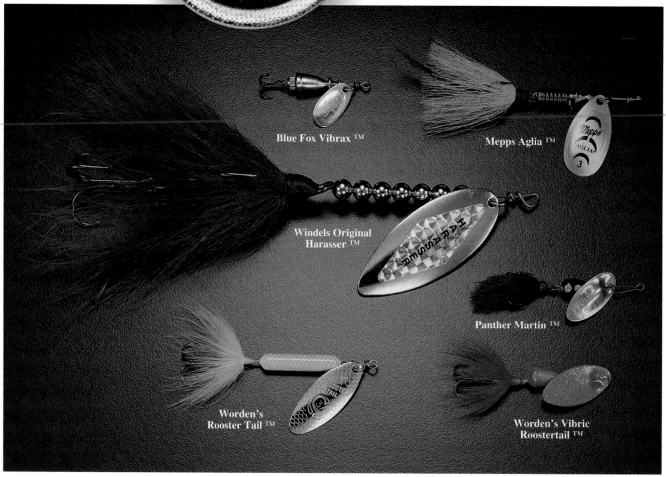

Blue Fox Vibrax ™

Mepps Aglia ™

Windels Original Harasser ™

Panther Martin ™

Worden's Rooster Tail ™

Worden's Vibric Roostertail ™

STANDARD SPINNERS come in two basic styles. The clevis type has a blade attached to a U-shaped metal clevis that rotates around the shaft. On the sonic type, the shaft runs directly through the blade. The body of a standard spinner is behind the blade and consists of an elongated piece of metal, or of metal or plastic beads. In addition to the body, most spinners also have a separate bead behind the blade to reduce friction.

A sonic-type spinner has a blade that spins directly on the shaft. The blade is concave on one end and convex on the other. A sonic blade starts rotating at a low retrieve speed. It has less water resistance than a blade mounted on a clevis, making the lure well suited to fishing in fast current.

Fishing with Standard Spinners

In a survey conducted by a national muskie-fishing club, large bucktail spinners accounted for more trophy muskies than any other lure. Big spinners work equally well for northern pike, and smaller versions excel for pickerel, trout, salmon and smallmouth bass.

When selecting spinners, the main consideration is overall length, from end of shaft to end of hook, including dressing. For small- to medium-sized trout, spinners should measure 1½ to 3 inches; for smallmouth and spotted bass, pickerel, salmon and large trout, 2½ to 4 inches; and for northern pike and muskies, 4 inches or longer.

The blade does not rotate as the lure sinks, so standard spinners generally work better when retrieved steadily than when jigged erratically. In some cases, you may have to twitch the lure to start the blade spinning.

If you reel a spinner at constant speed, fish will often follow without striking. But if you suddenly reel faster, they may grab the lure, thinking it is attempting to escape. Increasing the speed also makes the blade rotate faster, changing the pattern of vibrations and triggering uninterested fish.

When fishing a standard spinner in deep current, you may have to angle your casts upstream to reach the desired depth. If you cast downstream, the blade will spin too fast, giving the lure too much lift.

In shallow current, angle your casts downstream to prevent snagging. A standard spinner works well when drifted into hard-to-reach spots and allowed to hang in the current.

A major problem in fishing with standard spinners is keeping the blade turning freely. If the clevis becomes bent, it may bind on the shaft, slowing the rotation of the blade. Because standard spinners lack a safety-pin arm or tapered body in front, weeds and bits of algae tend to foul the blade.

Another problem is line twist. The shaft tends to revolve in the direction the blade spins. To minimize twisting, attach the spinner with a ball-bearing swivel. A clevis that is bent or fouled with weeds also causes line twist because water pressure against the fixed blade makes the entire lure spin.

You can also prevent line twist by selecting a spinner with a bent shaft or by bending the shaft ahead of the blade so it forms an angle of about 45 degrees. A bent shaft makes a swivel unnecessary.

Tips for Fishing with Standard Spinners

CHECK your spinner periodically to make sure the clevis is not bent or fouled with bits of vegetation. Straighten a bent clevis with a needlenose pliers.

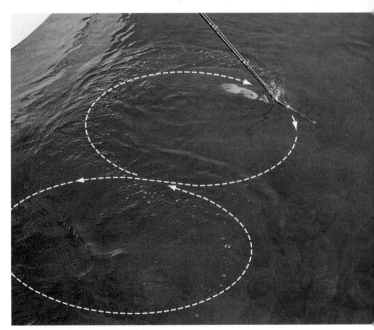

FIGURE-EIGHT a bucktail spinner at boatside if a muskie or northern pike follows it. Before beginning your figure-eight, push the free-spool button on your reel and thumb the line.

Weight-Forward Spinners

Charter-boat captains on Lake Erie rely almost exclusively on weight-forward spinners to locate walleye schools in the vast expanses of open water. These lures excel whenever fish are scattered over a large area or suspended at a certain depth.

Most weight-forward spinners also work well for fishing in deep water or fast current. They have narrow bodies that cause them to sink rapidly and hold their depth. Others are better suited to shallower water because their wider bodies give them a planing effect. Some models have a long wire shaft in front of the head to reduce the chances of a bite-off when fishing northern pike or muskies.

The lead body on a weight-forward spinner makes it easy to cast. The body is molded to the shaft and acts as a keel, preventing line twist. Because of the position of the weight, the lure sinks headfirst. The blade spins while the lure is dropping, attracting fish and tempting them to strike.

Weight-forward spinners are usually tipped with some type of live bait, so most come with a single hook. The hook is attached to ride with the point up, making the lure relatively snagless. Fishermen who use nightcrawlers often replace the single hook with a treble. The worm stays on the hook better and you will lose fewer fish.

Fishing with Weight-Forward Spinners

The fast-sinking design makes the weight-forward spinner a natural choice for bottom-hugging fish like walleyes. But these lures will also catch smallmouth and spotted bass, northern pike and trout. Because you can cast weight-forward spinners a long distance, they work well for reaching surface schools of white bass and stripers.

For small- to medium-sized trout, smallmouth and spotted bass and white bass, use weight-forward spinners from 1/8 to 3/8 ounce; for walleyes and large trout, 1/4 to 1/2 ounce; and for striped bass and northern pike, 1/2 to 1 ounce.

If cast improperly, weight-forward spinners tangle easily. The lure sails through the air headfirst, so the hook tends to catch on the line. To avoid this problem, use a soft lob cast rather than a snap cast. Stop the lure just before it hits the water. This will turn it around and prevent the hook from catching the line as the lure sinks.

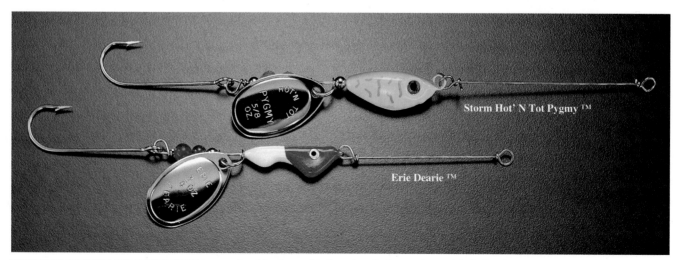

WEIGHT-FORWARD SPINNERS have a lead body molded to the shaft, a spinner blade behind the body and a single or treble hook with or without dressing. Most have a tapered head that slips through weeds.

To find the best depth, many fishermen use the countdown technique (p. 97). Weight-forward spinners are ideal for this method. They stay at a relatively constant depth when retrieved, so they remain in the fish zone longer than most other lures.

When you begin your retrieve, lift the rod tip sharply to start the blade turning. Begin reeling when you feel the resistance of the blade. Reel fast enough to keep the blade turning.

Weight-forward spinners work well when reeled steadily, but a darting retrieve may produce more fish. Periodically make a long sideways sweep with your rod, then bring your rod forward while reeling rapidly to keep the blade turning. Fish often strike just as the lure begins to accelerate.

Tie a weight-forward spinner directly to your line. Because the lure will not twist your line, you do not need a swivel. A snap or swivel increases the chances of fouling, because the lure can whip around on the cast.

Walleye and trout fishermen often tip weight-forward spinners with nightcrawlers. Pike anglers generally use minnows. Pork rind and soft plastic tails also work well for tipping.

How to Drift-fish with a Weight-forward Spinner

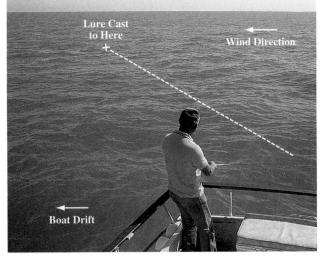

ANGLE your cast downwind as the boat drifts, then count the spinner down to the proper depth. Start your retrieve with your rod on the upwind side, holding your tip low and at an angle to the line.

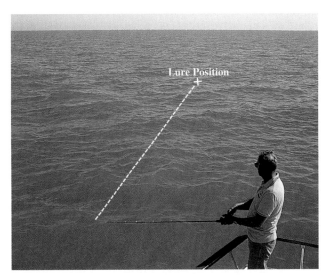

SWITCH your rod to the downwind side as the lure swings to the upwind side. Keep your rod tip low and at an angle to the line. Holding your rod at an angle increases your sensitivity, so you can detect subtle strikes.

Tips for Fishing with Weight-forward Spinners

CAST a weight-forward spinner tipped with a nightcrawler along brushy shorelines and retrieve slowly so the lure bumps the brushtops. The combination of noise, flash and scent will draw fish out of the tangle.

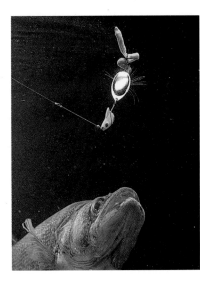

GLOB a nightcrawler on a weight-forward spinner so that no more than an inch of the worm trails behind the hook. Crawlers increase the buoyancy of the lure, enabling you to fish slowly just above bottom without snagging.

Spinnerbaits

Spinnerbaits were designed to solve the problems encountered by southern bass anglers in trying to fish reservoirs strewn with timber and brush. Standard or weight-forward spinners snag too easily under these conditions.

The shaft of a spinnerbait is bent in the shape of an open safety pin. The bent shaft prevents weeds and branches from fouling the hook and blade. Yet spinnerbaits hook fish better than most other weedless lures because the entire hook is exposed.

Many fishermen use spinnerbaits to locate fish in shallow water. You can cover a lot of water quickly and the flash and vibration draw strikes from the most aggressive fish. Even if a fish does not take the

Stanley Wedge ™

Mann's Classic Twin Spin ™

Johnson's Beetle Spin ™

Classic Hart Throb ™

M/G Muskie Tandem ™

SPINNERBAITS include the single spin, which has a single blade attached to the end of the upper arm with a barrel or snap-swivel; tandem spin, which is similar to a single spin, but has another blade on a clevis on the upper shaft; twin spin, which has two separate upper shafts, each with a single blade.

lure, it may follow and reveal its location. Then you can use a slower or less flashy lure to catch it.

When selecting spinnerbaits, consider the length of the upper arm, the thickness of the shaft and the shape of the head.

In most situations, use a spinnerbait with an upper arm long enough so that the blade rides above the hook point. Models with a shorter arm work best for helicoptering (p. 28). But if the arm is too short, it will not protect the hook from snags or provide enough stability to keep the lure from rolling. If the arm is too long, it will reduce your hooking percentage because fish often strike at the blade.

A thin-wire shaft transfers the vibration from the blade to the skirt for maximum wiggle. And thin wire enables you to hook fish more easily because it collapses on the strike. A thick-wire shaft is better in timber and brush because it deflects off branches. Most spinnerbaits have a pointed or bullet-shaped lead head molded to the lower shaft. The streamlined head helps the lure snake through weeds. Some small spinnerbaits have a detachable free-swinging jig instead of a fixed head. The jig is not as weedless, but hooks fish better.

Spinnerbaits come in single-blade, tandem-blade and twin-blade models. Single-blade types produce the strongest beat and helicopter well, making them a good all-around choice. Tandems have more water resistance, so they run shallower at a given retrieve speed and are effective for bulging the surface (p. 28). Twin-blade types are best in heavy cover because the dual upper shafts protect the hook better than a single shaft.

Most spinnerbaits have skirts of silicone, live rubber, bucktail, tinsel, Mylar® or marabou. But some, called *spin-rigs,* come without skirts and are intended for use with live bait or pork strips.

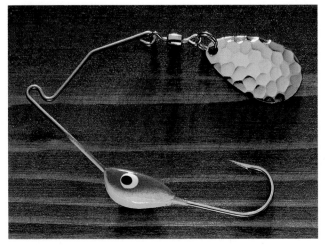

Spin-rig

Fishing with Spinnerbaits

Many professional bass anglers rely heavily on spinnerbaits for fishing the varied waters encountered on the tournament circuit. The spinnerbait's versatility makes it a good choice for a broad range of fishing situations.

A spinnerbait can be fished with many different retrieves. You can reel slowly along bottom, at moderate speed a few feet below the surface or fast enough so the lure bulges or breaks the surface. You can also hop a spinnerbait along bottom or jig it vertically around cover. Crappie fishermen even troll with spinnerbaits when searching for fish in open water. Experiment with different retrieves to find the one that is best for the conditions.

A properly tuned spinnerbait does not twist when retrieved, so you should tie it directly to your line. A snap or swivel will increase the chances of the lure tangling in the line.

If your spinnerbait has a coil of wire for an eye, your line may pass between the arms and wedge in the coil. If this happens, cut the line and retie it to eliminate the frayed mono. Spinnerbaits with an open slot for an eye will not catch the line.

TUNE a spinnerbait by bending the upper arm (arrow) to align with the hook (dotted line). A properly tuned spinnerbait runs with its blades on top.

Fishermen often fail to recognize strikes when using spinnerbaits. Fish commonly strike with only a gentle nudge. Whenever you detect a pause in the beat of the blade, set the hook.

Spinnerbaits often work better when tipped with a pork strip or live bait, particularly nightcrawlers and minnows. Some panfish anglers remove the soft plastic grub tails and substitute live grubs, worms, bits of shrimp or pieces of scent-impregnated fabric.

While spinnerbaits were designed primarily for catching largemouth bass, they also work well for smallmouth and spotted bass, crappies, sunfish, northern pike, pickerel and muskies. Spinnerbaits weighing 1/32 to 1/8 ounce work best for panfish, 1/8 to 3/8 ounce for smallmouth and spotted bass, 1/4 to 1 ounce for largemouths and pickerel and up to 3 ounces for large muskies and northerns.

Spinnerbait Retrieves

BULGE the surface with a spinnerbait by holding your rod tip high and reeling just fast enough so the blades do not quite break the surface. Bulging works best in warm water when fish feed actively in the shallows.

STOP-AND-GO retrieve is ideal for fishing around cover. You can bump the bait off the wood, allow it to flutter a little, then resume your retrieve, drawing the attention of any bass using the cover.

SHAKE a spinnerbait when there is no visible cover to deflect the bait and give it an erratic action; shake the rod tip rapidly as you reel. You don't need to shake as much in heavy timber or brush; the bait gets action from bouncing off the branches.

HELICOPTER a spinnerbait alongside vertical cover like a submerged tree. Keep your line taut to detect any change in the beat. Helicoptering works best in cold water or when sunlight drives fish into deep cover.

CAST a spinnerbait beyond an obstruction like a stump, then retrieve so that the lure bumps the cover. The momentary break in blade rotation often triggers a strike. The shady side of the cover is usually most productive.

Tips for Using Spinnerbaits

ASSEMBLE your own spinnerbaits from components. You can buy plain arms and add blades and lead-head jigs. Or you can buy arms with the heads molded on, then add blades, swivels and skirts.

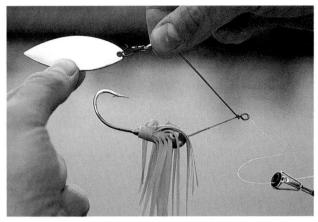

REPLACE the standard Colorado blade on your spinnerbait with a much larger willow-leaf blade. The willow-leaf blade has more flash and can be retrieved more rapidly, so it works better for locating active fish.

SHORTEN the upper arm to make a spinnerbait helicopter better. For best performance, the blade should ride ahead of the hook. To make the lure drop more slowly, use a larger blade.

ATTACH a trailer hook by sliding a small piece of rubber tubing over the end, then pushing the spinnerbait hook through the eye. The rubber keeps the stinger in line with the arms for protection from snags.

How to Add Flash to a Spinnerbait Skirt

REMOVE the skirt from a spinnerbait, open the O-ring with a longnose pliers and insert several strands of Mylar® or Flashabou™ (left). Trim them to the same length as the skirt, then replace the skirt. Flash from the reflective strips increases the bait's visibility (right), a big advantage in low-clarity water.

Buzzbaits

A hungry bass in the shallows finds it difficult to resist the splash and sputter of a buzzbait. Few other lures create as much surface disturbance.

All buzzbaits have a double- or triple-winged propeller, called a *buzzblade*. On some buzzbaits, the blade turns on a safety-pin shaft identical to that of a spinnerbait. On others, it turns on a straight shaft like that of a standard spinner.

The buzzblade is designed to operate half in and half out of the water, resulting in the gurgling surface action. Some buzzbaits have counter rotating twin blades for even more disturbance.

Because the buzzbait is designed only for surface fishing, it is not as versatile as the spinnerbait. But a buzzbait often works better than a spinnerbait for fishing over shallow, weedy flats. The buzzblade is less likely to foul in weeds or grass than an ordinary spinner blade. A buzzbait may also work better than a

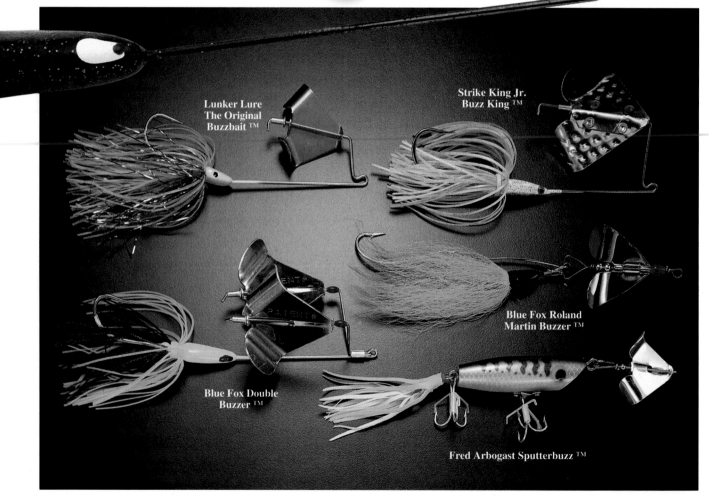

BUZZBAITS include safety-pin type with a buzzblade that rotates around the upper arm and straight type with a buzzblade that turns on the main shaft and a weedless hook. Both types may have double blades that rotate in opposite directions. Most buzzbaits come with skirts of silicone or bucktail.

spinnerbait in murky water. Even when fish cannot see the lure, they can hear the sound of the blade breaking water.

Buzzbaits work best in relatively calm water. If there is too much wave action, fish do not seem to notice the surface disturbance from the lure.

Some fishermen tip their buzzbaits with soft plastics or pork strips for extra action. These attractors also add buoyancy to the lure. But if the attractor trails too far behind the hook, fish will often strike short.

Fishing with Buzzbaits

Buzzbaits have gained a reputation as one of the best shallow-water lures for largemouth bass. But many fishermen do not realize that these lures also work well for northern pike, pickerel and muskies.

For largemouth bass and pickerel, use buzzbaits from 1/4 to 5/8 ounce; for northern pike and muskies, from 5/8 to 1 ounce.

When fishing for bass, reel a buzzbait steadily, just fast enough to keep it on the surface. For pike, muskies and pickerel, a faster retrieve is usually more productive. Fishing in slop usually requires a slower retrieve than fishing in open water or sparse vegetation. Dense overhead weeds make it difficult for a fish to zero in on a fast-moving lure.

When a slow retrieve is needed, select a twin-bladed buzzbait or one with a wide, spoon-type body. The twin blades give the lure more lift, and the flattened body keeps it planing on the surface. The choice of safety-pin versus in-line styles depends mostly on personal preference.

To keep your lure on the surface, stop it just before it hits the water. This removes the slack from your line so you can start your retrieve before the lure has a chance to sink. While retrieving, hold your rod tip high enough so that your lure stays on the surface, but not so high that you cannot set the hook.

Fish are sometimes difficult to hook with buzzbaits. Because of dense cover, they may have trouble catching the lure. They splash or swirl nearby but miss the hook. Wait until you see or feel the fish grab the lure before you set the hook.

To improve your chances of hooking fish, add a trailer hook. Rig a long-shaft single hook so the point rides up, and secure it exactly the same way as recommended for spinnerbaits (p. 29). In open water, use a treble hook for the trailer.

Buzzbaits work especially well in spring, when largemouths are spawning on shallow, weedy flats. Cast beyond a nest, then reel the lure directly over it. Later in the season, buzzbaits work best on calm mornings or evenings, on overcast days or at night, the times when most predator fish prowl weedy or brushy shallows.

Do not hesitate to cast a buzzbait into the thickest, most impenetrable cover, especially in hot weather. Few lures are more effective for drawing fish from beneath the slop.

Tips for Fishing with Buzzbaits

TUNE your buzzbait on the way to the lake by experimenting with different ways of bending the blade, then holding the lure out the car window. When the blade spins fastest, the lure is properly tuned.

BEND the blade arm slightly downward so that as the blade rotates, it just ticks the shaft. The extra noise may attract more fish. Avoid bending the arm so much that the blade cannot turn rapidly.

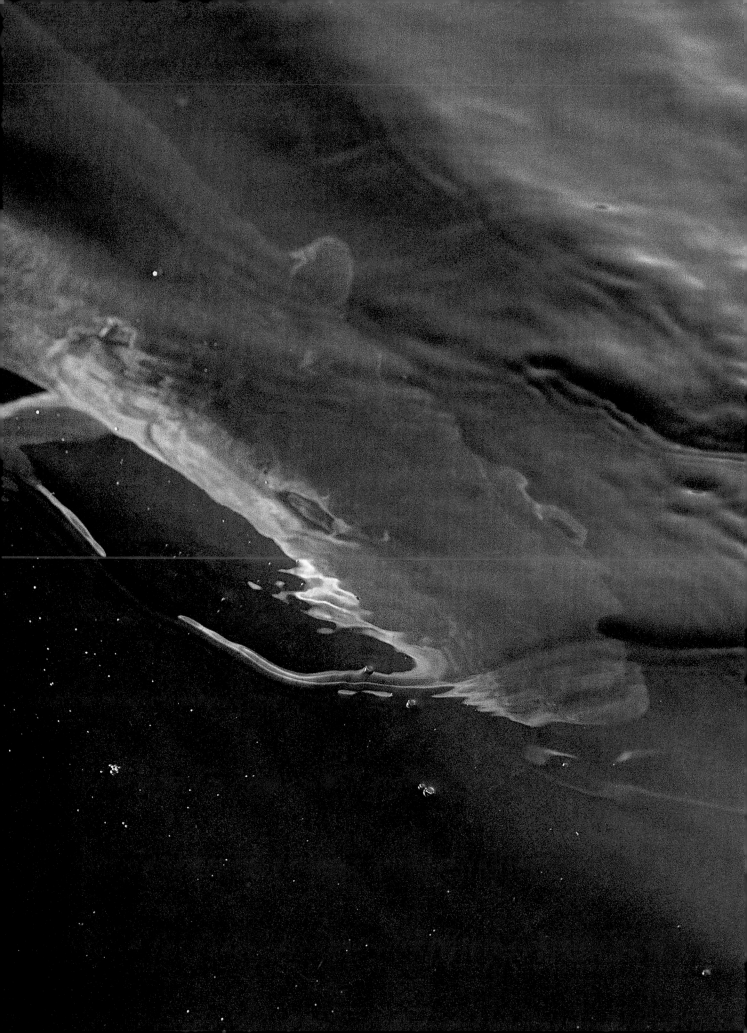

Plugs

Plugs

Originally, the term *plug* referred to a lure carved from a block of wood. Many fishermen still consider wooden plugs the best, but most modern plugs are made of hollow plastic or hard foamed plastic.

Plastic plugs are less expensive and hold their finish better than wooden plugs. Plastic plugs of a given model are more consistent in shape, density and action than wooden ones. But wooden plugs sometimes have a better action than similar ones made of plastic. A balsa minnow, for example, wobbles more readily than a plastic minnow of the same size and shape.

Most plugs imitate baitfish, but some resemble animals like mice, frogs and crayfish. Other plugs attract fish by their action and flash, resembling nothing in particular. All plugs produce some sound that draws the attention of gamefish. It may be a high- or low-frequency vibration; a pop, gurgle or splash; or merely the sound of the hooks clinking on the hook hangers. Some plugs also have chambers filled with shot that produce a loud rattle.

Some plugs are designed exclusively for surface fishing. Surface plugs work especially well when fish are spawning or feeding in shallow water. But they will sometimes draw fish up from deeper water.

Surface plugs are most effective at water temperatures of 60°F or warmer. The water must be relatively calm; otherwise, fish do not seem to notice the action. Surface plugs generally work best in early morning, at dusk or at night, although they may catch fish any time of day. They fall into the following categories:

Stickbait — These long, slender, floating plugs lack lips or propellers. They have no built-in wobble, so the fisherman must supply the action.

Propbait — Similar to stickbaits, these lures have a propeller at one or both ends.

Crawler — A large faceplate or wings on the sides make the lure crawl across the surface when retrieved steadily. Crawlers produce a plopping or gurgling sound.

Chugger — The indented face catches water when the plug is jerked across the surface, producing a popping or chugging noise. Some chuggers have a slow, swimming action when retrieved steadily.

Subsurface plugs run at depths of 1 to 20 feet or more. These plugs are much more versatile than surface plugs. They work well in either calm or rough water and will catch fish at any time of day. You can select either shallow- or deep-running models, depending on the depth of the fish. Subsurface plugs fall into these categories:

Crankbait — Most crankbaits float at rest, but some sink and others are neutrally buoyant. All have a lip, which makes them dive and wiggle when retrieved.

Minnow plug — Like crankbaits, these plugs have lips and may float, sink or be neutrally buoyant. Designed to imitate thin-bodied baitfish, minnow plugs have a side-to-side wobble.

Vibrating crankbait — These thin-bodied plugs do not have lips. The attachment eye is on top of the head, resulting in a tight wiggle. Most vibrating crankbaits sink, but a few float while at rest.

Trolling plug — Designed primarily or exclusively for trolling, these plugs generally have a large flattened forehead that creates a wide, erratic wobble. Trolling plugs are difficult to cast because they are relatively light, and their shape is too wind-resistant. Most trolling plugs float at rest.

Jerkbait — These large, elongated plugs are intended mainly for catching muskies and large pike. Most float at rest, dive when given a strong jerk, then float back to the surface. Many have metal tails that can be bent to change the action.

Plugs range in size from the tiny, inch-long models used for panfish to the huge, foot-long plugs intended for muskies. When selecting plugs, length is a more important consideration than weight. Following are plug lengths most commonly used for various types of gamefish.

SPECIES	PLUG LENGTH
Crappies	1 to 2 inches
Small to medium trout	1 to 3 inches
White bass	½ to 3 inches
Smallmouth and spotted bass	2 to 3 inches
Largemouth bass and pickerel	2 to 6 inches
Walleyes	3 to 6 inches
Salmon and large trout	3 to 7 inches
Northern pike, muskies and stripers	4 to 12 inches

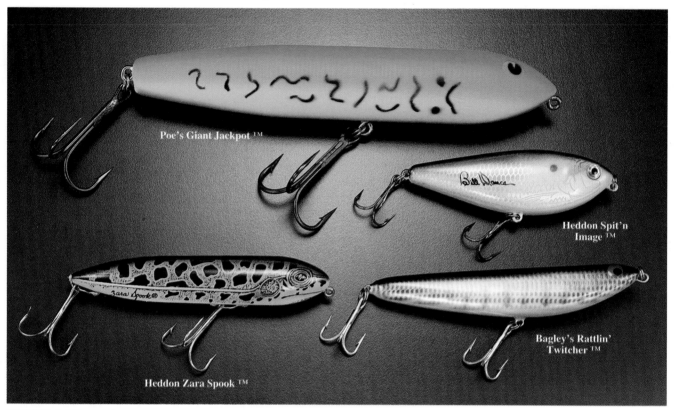

STICKBAITS consist of a long body, usually tapered at each end, with extra weight at the rear. The attachment eye is at the nose.

Stickbaits

A stickbait walked noisily across the surface will draw gamefish from deep water better than any other surface lure. In clear water, fish may rush the lure from 15 feet down.

Stickbaits rank among the top lures for big largemouths, but they also work well for smallmouth and spotted bass, white and striped bass, pickerel, northern pike and muskies.

The basic stickbait retrieve is called *walking-the-dog.* Because of the way it is balanced, a stickbait will move in an alternating left-right-left manner when retrieved

with short, sharp jerks. This action mimics a crippled minnow struggling on the surface.

With a little practice, you can walk a stickbait to one side, enabling you to reach cover to the right or left of your retrieve path.

Fish often bulge or swirl the surface near a stickbait without grabbing the lure. Wait until you actually feel a tug before setting the hook.

A fast-action rod with a springy tip works best for walking-the-dog because it enables you to twitch the lure sharply. Stickbaits work best when fished

How to Walk-the-Dog

CAST a stickbait over submerged weeds or brush, then give it a sharp twitch (left), letting your line go slack while the lure skids to one side. As soon as the lure stops, twitch again (right) and let the line go slack while the lure skids in the other direction. Continue twitching to make the lure walk in a zigzag fashion. To walk the lure to one side, make jerks in rapid succession rather than waiting for the lure to stop between jerks.

with relatively light line, usually from 8- to 10-pound test. Light line allows the lure to move from side to side easily. Like other surface lures, stickbaits should be tied directly to the line, without snaps or leaders. For pike or muskies, use a wire leader no heavier than necessary to hold the fish.

Propbaits

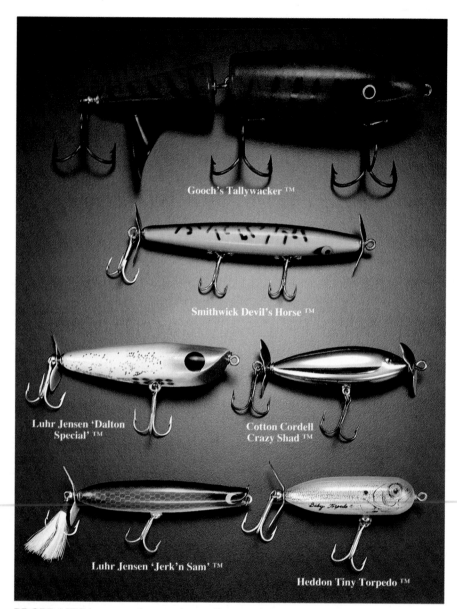

Gooch's Tallywacker ™

Smithwick Devil's Horse ™

Luhr Jensen 'Dalton Special' ™

Cotton Cordell Crazy Shad ™

Luhr Jensen 'Jerk'n Sam' ™

Heddon Tiny Torpedo ™

PROPBAITS have an elongated, usually unweighted body, and an attachment eye at the nose. Some models have a propeller at one end, and others have propellers at both ends.

Propbaits are the most versatile of all surface lures. You can fish small spots thoroughly with a twitching retrieve or cover large areas by reeling rapidly. And propbaits create more disturbance than most other surface lures, so they work well even when wind ripples the surface.

A slow, twitching retrieve generally works best for largemouth, smallmouth and spotted bass; a fast, steady retrieve works for pike, muskies, stripers and white bass. A few propbaits have a weight in the rear, so they can be fished with a walk-the-dog retrieve.

Some propbaits have a flattened or dished face, resulting in a more erratic action than models with a pointed nose. Models with a propeller on each end create the most disturbance and work best for fast retrieves. On some brands, the twin props counter rotate to prevent the entire lure from spinning.

The tackle used with propbaits is similar to that used with stickbaits. And like stickbaits, propbaits are usually tied directly to the line. If you use a heavy snap and leader, the nose may run below the surface, preventing the propellers from throwing water.

Tips for Fishing with Propbaits

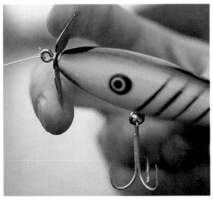

TUNE the blades if they do not spin rapidly. Adjust the angle by bending the blades backward (above) or forward; the pitch by twisting them.

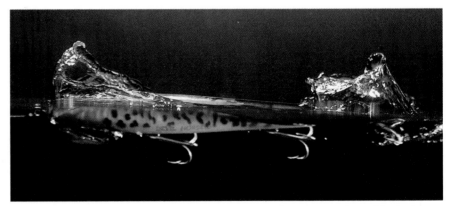

TWITCH a propbait with slack line for the best action. By starting with slack line, you can jerk the lure more sharply than you could with a taut line, yet the lure will move only a few inches. Continue retrieving in short twitches followed by pauses until the lure pulls away from the cover.

39

Crawlers

Crawlers excel when exploring for fish in large expanses of shallow water. They work best with a steady, moderately fast retrieve, enabling you to cover a lot of area quickly.

Many largemouth bass fishermen rate crawlers among the best lures for night fishing. The continuous plopping sound makes it easy to monitor the lure's location. And with a steady retrieve, the line stays taut so you can detect strikes. Crawlers also work well for northern pike, pickerel and muskies.

Models with a faceplate will swim through sparse weeds without fouling. But hinged-arm models tend to collect bits of weeds or algae at the arm joints.

The speed at which you retrieve a crawler is critical. Too fast, and the plug will skim the surface with little action. Too slow, and it will not produce the gurgling sound. The best speed is that which produces the most pronounced wobble and the loudest gurgle.

If fish do not strike with a steady retrieve, try adding an occasional pause and twitch. Or stop reeling periodically and let the ripples subside.

Hi - Fin Creeper ™

Heddon Crazy Crawler ™

JITTERBUG

Fred Arbogast Jitterbug ™

CRAWLERS have either a wide cupped faceplate or arms, which are usually collapsible, on the sides of the body. All crawlers have relatively stocky bodies and attachment eyes at the front. The force of water alternately pushing on one side of the face or one arm, then the other, produces the wide wobble.

How to Make Crawlers More Weedless

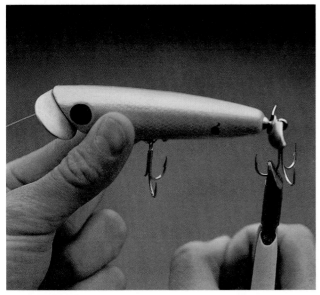

POSITION the treble hooks so that only one point of each hook aims forward, then cut off the front points. The hooks ride with points up and slide easily over weeds.

SECURE the side trebles on a Musky Jitterbug® above the body with a rubber band, wire or heavy monofilament. Or remove the side trebles from the lure.

Chuggers

A chugger could be described as an overgrown fly-rod popper. Like poppers used for fly fishing, chuggers have a scooped-out, grooved or flattened face that makes a popping or chugging sound when the lure is twitched.

Generally considered largemouth bass lures, chuggers will also catch smallmouth and spotted bass as well as stripers. They are not as effective as other surface lures for pike and muskies.

Chuggers work better than most other surface lures for fishing precise targets. To fish a small opening in a bed of lily pads, for example, cast a chugger into the spot and wait for the ripples to die. Often, fish will strike almost immediately. If not, give the lure a twitch, moving it forward only an inch or so. Then wait for the ripples to die again. If nothing strikes after two or three twitches, cast to another opening.

How hard you twitch a chugger depends on the mood of the fish. Jerking too hard creates an explosion of water, causing the fish to spook. A moderate twitch usually works better; at times, fish prefer a gentle twitch that barely disturbs the surface.

Fishing small pockets is more difficult with a chugger than with a fly-rod popper. With fly-fishing tackle, you can place the lure more accurately and lift it off the water without catching weeds. To make a chugger more weedless, trim the front point of each treble (p. 41).

Pinpoint casting is important when using a chugger. A slow- or medium-action rod enables you to cast more accurately than a fast-action rod. In dense-cover situations, use line from 12- to 20-pound test. Otherwise, 8- to 10-pound line is adequate.

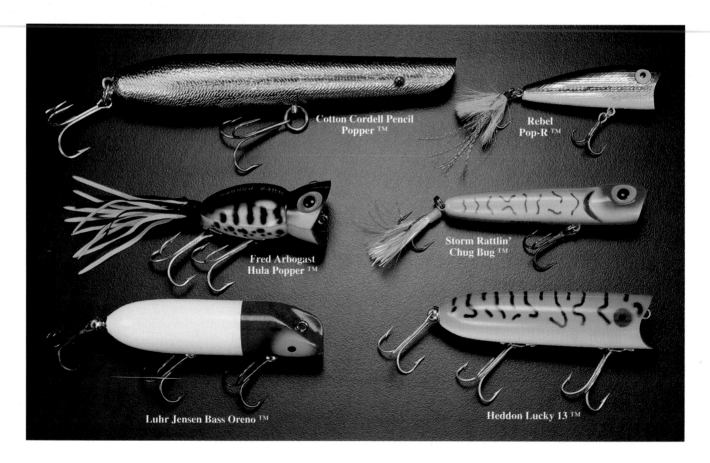

Cotton Cordell Pencil Popper ™

Rebel Pop-R ™

Fred Arbogast Hula Popper ™

Storm Rattlin' Chug Bug ™

Luhr Jensen Bass Oreno ™

Heddon Lucky 13 ™

Tips for Fishing with Chuggers

TIE a small jig to the rear hook of a chugger to catch white bass, stripers or other surface schooling fish. The chugger provides casting weight and creates a surface disturbance, increasing the effectiveness of the jig.

WORK a grooved-face chugger beneath the surface to imitate an injured baitfish. Point your rod at the lure and reel until the head dips underwater. Then jerk repeatedly while reeling to give the lure a darting action.

Crankbaits

Fishermen use the term *crankbait* for any lure with a lip that causes it to dive and wiggle when cranked in. Designed primarily for casting, most crankbaits have a relatively short, aerodynamic body. Minnow plugs are sometimes classed as crankbaits, but will be considered a separate category in this book.

Crankbaits work best at water temperatures of 55°F or warmer. At cooler temperatures, fish usually refuse to chase fast-moving lures.

Because you can cast a crankbait a long distance and retrieve it rapidly, you can cover a lot of water quickly. Even when fish are not actively feeding, the intense wiggle often triggers strikes. And when fish are feeding, more will see your plug than would see a lure that moves more slowly.

Most crankbaits float at rest, but a few sink, enabling you to count them down to the desired depth before beginning your retrieve. Some are neutrally buoyant, and suspend when you stop the retrieve.

Crankbaits are made of foamed or hard plastic or wood, usually balsa or cedar. Hard plastic crankbaits generally cast better than foamed plastic or wooden ones of a similar design, but they do not wiggle as well on a slow retrieve.

The type of lip determines how deep a crankbait will dive. Many fishermen believe that a crankbait with a steeply sloping lip dives the deepest. But in reality, one with a lip extending straight off the front runs deeper. The size of the lip in comparison to the body also affects the running depth. The longer and wider the lip, the deeper the lure will dive. Crankbaits with small, steeply sloping lips may run as shallow as a foot; those with large, straight lips, as deep as 20 feet. Some deep divers will reach depths of 30 feet or more when trolled on a long line.

Shallow-running crankbaits work best for fishing on shallow flats or over submerged weeds or brush. Deep divers would dig into the bottom or foul quickly under these circumstances. But deep divers are better suited for fishing deep structure, like a sharply sloping shoreline. For extremely deep water, use a sinking crankbait.

Some crankbaits have metal lips that can be bent to make the lure run deeper or shallower. But the majority of crankbaits have fixed lips that cannot be adjusted. Most fishermen carry a selection of crankbaits with different types of lips, so they can fish at different depths.

The lip on a crankbait serves another important purpose. Most crankbaits run in a head-down posi-

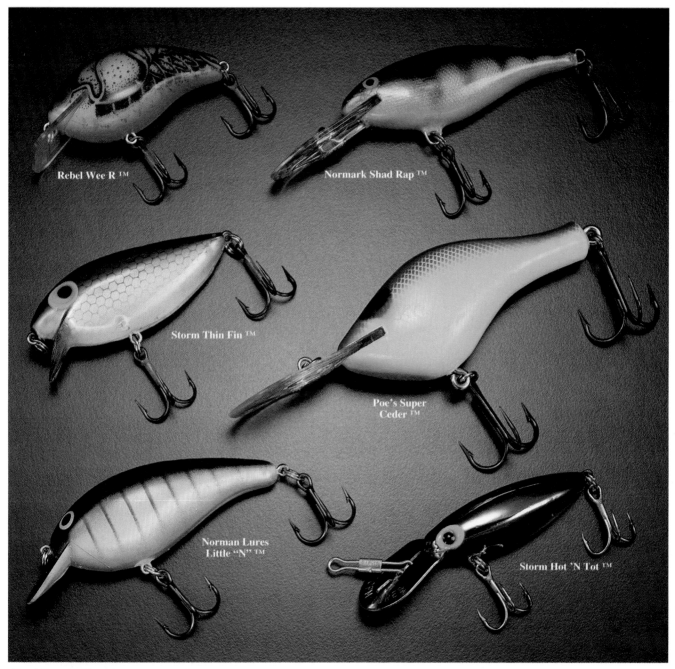

CRANKBAITS include shallow runners with small, steeply sloping lips and attachment eyes at the nose and deep divers with large, straight lips and attachment eyes on the lip.

tion, so the lip contacts obstructions before the hooks do. As a result, the lure usually deflects off solid objects such as rocks and logs before the hooks can become snagged.

Fishing with Crankbaits

Some fishermen argue that crankbait fishing is boring because all you have to do is cast out and reel in. But anyone who has shared a boat with an expert crankbait fisherman knows better.

You must select a crankbait that runs at the proper depth. To determine how deep a crankbait tracks, retrieve the lure through water of a known depth, feeling for it to touch bottom. If it does, move to slightly deeper water and try again. Continue until the lure no longer touches, then note the depth.

Many fishermen believe that the faster you retrieve a crankbait, the deeper it will dive. Actually, every crankbait has an optimum speed at which it performs best. Too slow, and it will not dive or wiggle properly. Too fast, and it will turn sideways and lose depth.

RIP a crankbait through broadleaf weeds to catch pike, muskies or bass. The interruption in the plug's action often triggers a strike. Or bounce the plug off a stump or other obstruction.

Experiment with different retrieves to find the speed at which the lure tracks the deepest.

A crankbait will not attain maximum depth unless tuned so that it tracks perfectly straight. Depending on the type of lip, a crankbait must be tuned by bending or twisting the eye, bending the lip itself or bending the attachment wire.

Experienced crankbait fishermen sometimes mis-tune their crankbaits intentionally to make them run to the side. By mistuning your plug, you can fish beneath overhead cover like a dock or bump your plug into vertical cover like a seawall.

To reach maximum depth with a crankbait, cast as far as possible and keep your rod tip low while retrieving. With a shorter cast or higher rod position, you will begin pulling the plug upward before it reaches its potential depth.

Line diameter also affects how deep your crankbait runs. Thin line has less water resistance and allows the plug to run deeper than thick line. The smaller the plug, the more it is affected by line diameter.

When fishing a crankbait in open water or light cover, 8- to 12-pound mono is usually adequate. But you may need mono up to 25-pound test for fishing in heavy cover. Spinning tackle works well for shallow-running plugs or deep divers that do not pull too hard. But bait casting tackle is better for deep-diving plugs that have a lot of water resistance.

How to Tune Different Crankbaits

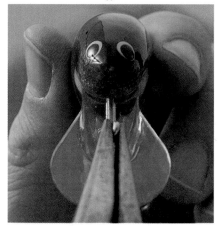

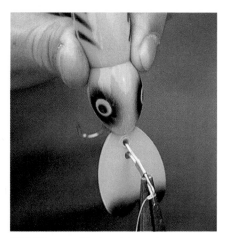

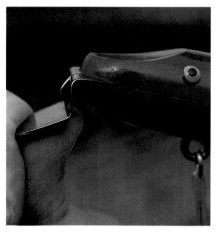

BEND or turn the attachment eye if the plug tracks to the side. If the plug tracks to the left, bend the eye to the right and vice versa.

TUNE a crankbait with a wire connecting arm by bending the wire in the same direction you would bend the eye on an ordinary crankbait.

ADJUST the angle of the metal lip to change the running depth. Bending the lip down makes the lure run shallower but wiggle more.

Techniques for Fishing with Crankbaits

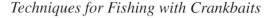

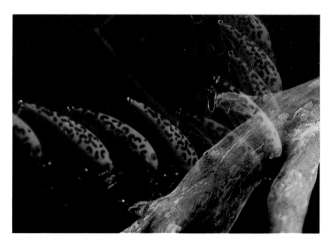

BUMP a crankbait along bottom by continuing to reel rapidly even after feeling bottom contact. The combination of noise, erratic action and stirred-up bottom debris often draws strikes from uninterested fish.

UNSNAG a floating, deep-diving crankbait by letting the line go slack if the lure catches in timber. The lure will float upward and backward, freeing itself. Some anglers remove the front treble to make the lure more snag-free.

For the best action, tie a crankbait directly to your line. If the plug does not have a split-ring on the eye, use a Duncan loop (p. 12). A heavy leader or snap-swivel will restrict the plug's wobble.

To keep your lure in the fish zone as long as possible, cast parallel to the structure or cover. For example, to work the shady side of a log, cast parallel to the log and retrieve the lure along its length. If you cast perpendicular to the log, your lure will be in the fish zone only a fraction of the time.

The way you retrieve a crankbait depends on the water temperature and the mood of the fish. In cool water or when fish are reluctant to strike, a stop-and-go retrieve usually works best. Fish often strike when you stop reeling and the lure starts to float upward. In warm water or when fish are actively feeding, a fast, steady retrieve is most effective.

When a fish grabs a crankbait it often hooks itself. But strikes can be much more subtle. If the fish hits while moving in the same direction as the lure, you will feel only a slight slackening of the line. Set the hook whenever you feel a change in the action.

Crankbaits will catch practically any type of gamefish except the smallest panfish species. Mini-crankbaits, measuring only about one inch in length, work well for good-sized panfish.

Minnow Plugs

Minnow plugs have a shape and swimming action remarkably similar to those of shiners or other slim-bodied baitfish.

Because minnow plugs rely mainly on their visual appeal to attract fish, they work best in relatively clear water. They do not produce as much sound as crankbaits or vibrating plugs, so they are less effective in waters of low clarity.

Minnow plugs generally have smaller lips than crankbaits, so the head does not swing as far to the side when the plug swims. The tight rocking action is less violent than the action of a crankbait, but much more lifelike.

Originally, minnow plugs were hand-carved from balsa wood. Many are still made of balsa, but some are now molded from plastic. Because of their light weight, balsa models wobble more than plastic ones. But they are harder to cast and less durable.

Most minnow plugs float at rest, but some are neutrally buoyant and others sink. The majority of floaters and neutrally buoyant plugs run shallow, from 1 to 5 feet below the surface, although some have very long lips and dive as deep as 12 feet or more.

Floating and neutrally buoyant minnow plugs rank among the top lures for casting or trolling along

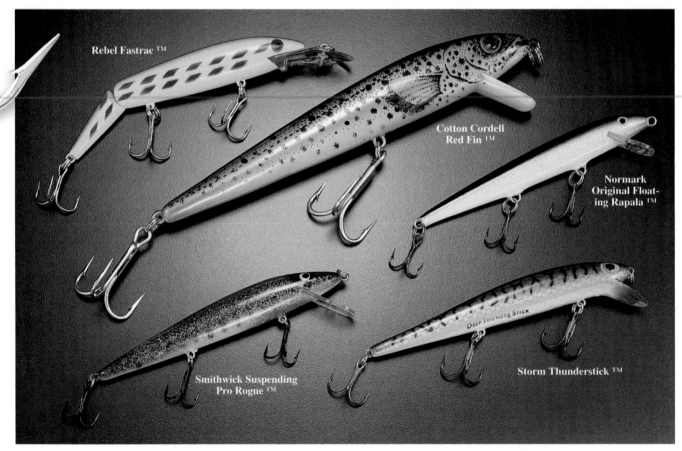

Rebel Fastrac ™

Cotton Cordell Red Fin ™

Normark Original Floating Rapala ™

Smithwick Suspending Pro Rogue ™

DEEP THUNDER STICK

Storm Thunderstick ™

MINNOW PLUGS include balsa and plastic models. Both have attachment eyes on the nose, and plastic or metal lips. Many balsa plugs have an internal wire connecting the attachment eye to the hooks. The wire insures that the hooks will not pull out of the soft wood, allowing the fish to escape.

shallow shorelines, over shallow reefs or above the tops of submerged weeds. Floaters can also be twitched erratically across the surface. Both work extremely well at night. Fish can easily see the silhouette of the shallow-running plug against the surface. Sinking models can be counted down to any depth, but they have less wobbling action than floaters.

Fishing with Minnow Plugs

The effectiveness of minnow plugs is not surprising because most gamefish prefer thin-bodied baitfish to those with deeper bodies. Baitfish with slim bodies are easier to swallow and less likely to lodge in a predator's throat.

Minnow plugs appeal to almost all gamefish, with the exception of small panfish. They work best for large-mouth, smallmouth and spotted bass; walleyes; northern pike, muskies and pickerel; stripers and trout.

To maximize the action of minnow plugs, you will need to attach them properly. A loop knot or small, round-nosed snap works best. Before casting, check the hooks to make sure that they are hanging straight. If they are cocked in the hook hangers, the plug will not run true.

Because of their light weight, floating minnow plugs are difficult to cast. For maximum casting distance, use spinning tackle and the lightest line practical for the conditions. Light line also allows the lure to wiggle more freely. Bait casting tackle can be used with sinking and large floating minnow plugs.

When casting a floating minnow plug in the shallows, use the wind to your advantage for maximum distance. When trolling in shallow water, let out a lot of line, up to 150 feet. Long-distance casting and long-line trolling reduce the chances of fish spooking when they see you or your boat. Unlike most crankbaits, floating minnow plugs will continue to run shallow despite the long length of line, so they are less likely to foul.

To work a floating minnow on the surface, cast it into a likely spot, then retrieve it with sharp twitches. Pause a few seconds after each twitch, as you would when fishing with a popper or chugger.

You can fish a sinking minnow plug on bottom by allowing it to sink until the line goes slack before beginning your retrieve. Reel just fast enough so that the lure bumps bottom occasionally. For suspended fish, count down a sinking minnow plug to the proper depth, just as you would count down a spoon (p. 97).

In most situations where a sinking minnow plug works well, a floating minnow plug will work even better. Attach a bottom-walker or pinch-on sinker ahead of the plug to reach the desired depth. The floating plug has a more attractive action and is less likely to snag because it rides farther off bottom.

A neutrally buoyant minnow plug can be retrieved much more slowly and still maintain its depth. Slower retrieves often work better in cool water or when fish are sluggish. A standard floating minnow plug must be retrieved at moderate speed to prevent it from rising quickly to the surface.

Tips for Fishing with Minnow Plugs

BEND the attachment eye to change the action of a minnow plug. Bend the eye downward for more wiggle; upward for less.

COAT damaged areas on the surface of a balsa minnow plug with fingernail polish. Otherwise, the wood will soak up water, ruining the plug's action.

CHANGE the silver finish on a minnow plug to another color with an indelible marking pen. The finish will retain its reflective quality.

Vibrating Crankbaits

The tight wiggle of a vibrating crankbait creates high-frequency sound waves that attract fish even in cool or murky water. Vibrating crankbaits work best for largemouth, smallmouth and spotted bass; northern pike; walleyes; white bass; and stripers.

Because most vibrating crankbaits sink rapidly, they offer optional presentations. Without changing lures, you can retrieve along bottom in deep water, count down to suspended fish or start retrieving immediately after the cast to catch fish near the surface. Vibrating crankbaits work well with a steady retrieve, but a darting retrieve varies the frequency of the vibrations and may trigger more strikes.

These crankbaits lack lips, so they are not as snag-resistant as standard crankbaits. They work well in open water or along the edges of weeds, brush or timber. But they can snag in dense cover.

These baits are ideal for covering a lot of water quickly. The narrow body has little wind or water resistance. This design and the weight of the plug allow long-distance casts. A rapid retrieve causes shot pellets in the sound chamber to vibrate and signal fish.

For maximum performance, tie the lure directly to the split-ring. A sensitive rod helps detect changes in the vibration that could signal a strike or indicate that the plug has become fouled.

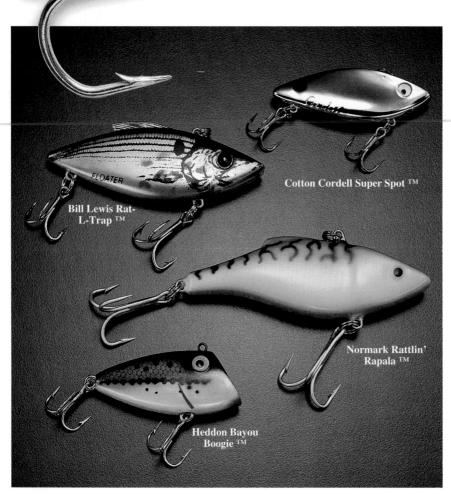

Cotton Cordell Super Spot ™

Bill Lewis Rat-L-Trap ™

FLOATER

Normark Rattlin' Rapala ™

Heddon Bayou Boogie ™

VIBRATING CRANKBAITS have an attachment eye on the back, causing the plug to run with its head angled down. Water pressure on the forehead produces the tight vibrating action.

Tips for Fishing with Vibrating Crankbaits

USE a vibrating crankbait that floats for fishing around shallow cover or for surface-schooling fish. Retrieve with your rod tip low, alternately reeling to draw the lure under the surface, then pausing so it floats back up.

FREE a snagged plug with a specially designed aluminum pole. Place your line inside the wire pigtail (inset). Then, with the line tight, slide the pole down until the pigtail hits the plug.

Trolling Plugs

Trolling plugs differ greatly in appearance and action but share one common feature: their design makes them difficult to cast. Many have too much wind resistance, some tangle too easily and others are simply too heavy.

Most trolling plugs have broad, flat foreheads that produce an exceptionally wide wobble. Some have lips or scooped-out heads that give them a narrower, crankbait-like wobble. A few have flattened faces, resulting in an erratic, darting action.

Fishermen generally use trolling plugs to cover large open-water areas. Trolling plugs are not suited for working a target precisely, because it is difficult to control their path unless trolling with a short line.

When selecting trolling plugs, consider the depth at which they run and the speed at which they have the best action.

If the fish are located within 20 feet of the surface, you can choose a trolling plug that runs at the proper depth with no added weight. The best way to determine exactly how deep a plug will run is to test it yourself. Few plugs run deeper than 20 feet, so you will need sinkers, drop weights, downriggers or diving planes to reach fish below that depth.

The speed and action fish prefer change from season to season and sometimes even from day to day. For consistent success, your plug selection must change accordingly. Experienced trollers generally carry a selection that includes speed-trolling plugs, which attain their best action at speeds from 5 to 7 mph; slow-trolling plugs, which reach peak performance at only 1 to 2 mph; and plugs that operate best at intermediate speeds.

Fishing with Trolling Plugs

Trolling with plugs may not be the most exciting fishing method ever devised, but it is certainly one of the deadliest. Trolling is the best technique for exploring open water and enables you to keep your plug at a selected depth indefinitely.

Because they work best in open water, trolling plugs are most effective for salmon, trout and striped bass. When fished along edges of cover, such as weedlines, trolling plugs will also take walleyes, bass, northern pike and muskies.

If you simply let out your line and motor about at random, you stand little chance of catching fish. Plan your trolling route so that your plug seldom strays away from likely cover, structure or a precise temperature layer.

Fishermen use a wide variety of electronic aids to help them catch fish with trolling plugs. Electronic depth finders are invaluable for determining the proper depth. Try fishing at different levels and note the depth immediately when you hook a fish. Chances are there will be more fish at the same level.

A water temperature gauge helps locate fish, like salmon and trout, that have very specific water temperature preferences. You will greatly improve your

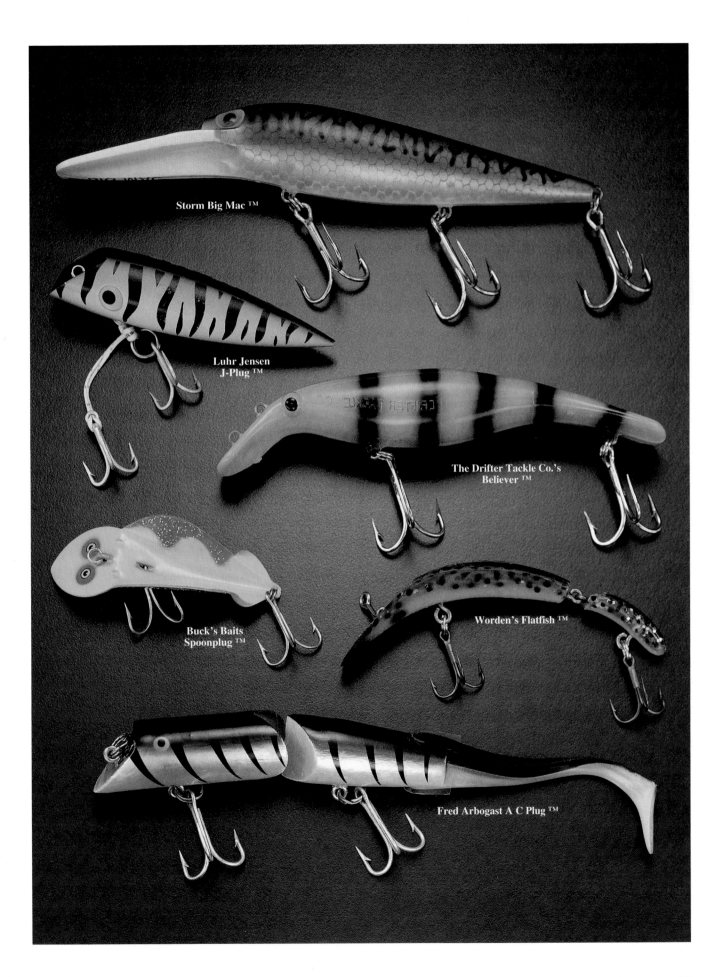

Storm Big Mac ™

Luhr Jensen
J-Plug ™

The Drifter Tackle Co.'s
Believer ™

Buck's Baits
Spoonplug ™

Worden's Flatfish ™

Fred Arbogast A C Plug ™

odds of catching fish by keeping your lure in the preferred temperature layer.

Trolling speed indicators help you keep your plug moving at the speed that produces the best action.

Downrigger fishermen sometimes use sophisticated water temperature-trolling speed monitors that provide readings at the depth the lures are running. Readings taken at the depth of the lures are more meaningful than surface readings. Temperatures at a particular depth often change dramatically as you troll. And currents on the surface may differ greatly from those in the depths, giving you a false idea of how fast your lure is moving.

Many anglers make the mistake of trolling too far off bottom in an effort to avoid snags. Unless fish are suspended in a specific temperature layer, you will usually draw more strikes by trolling deep enough to make your plug dig sand or bounce off rocks.

Another common mistake is trolling at the same speed regardless of the plug. Different plugs run best at different speeds, and the only sure way to find the best speed is to experiment. When using multiple lines, remember to use plugs designed to run at the same speed.

Multiple lines enable you to compare different actions, colors and sizes. If one plug begins to produce, attach similar plugs to all the other lines.

Trolling rods should be stiff enough to withstand the strong pull of the plug, but they need not be sensitive. Downrigger rods should be at least 7½ feet long and flexible enough to bend into the set position. Speed-trolling rods should be very stiff and no more than 5½ feet long. Level-wind reels are a better choice than spinning reels for most trolling situations. They minimize line twist and make it easier to return your plug to the right depth.

How to Use a Water Temperature-Trolling Speed Monitor

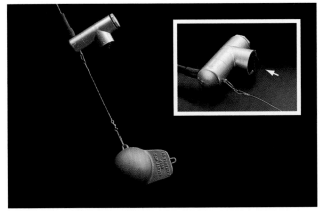

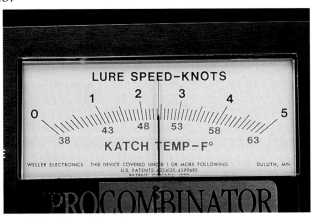

LOWER your cannonball to the desired depth with the sensor (inset) on the cable. The front face of the sensor measures temperature and the impeller (arrow) measures lure speed at the depth you are fishing.

WATCH the meter closely when trolling. If the water temperature changes, adjust your fishing depth to find the right temperature. You may have to speed up or slow down your motor to maintain a constant lure speed.

Other Ways to Maintain the Proper Trolling Speed

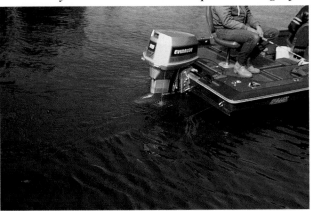

TIE a 6-foot piece of line to the back of the boat and attach a pilot plug identical to the one you are using. Watch the action of the pilot plug to determine if you are trolling at the right speed.

CHECK your speed with an electric trolling speed indicator. The meter measures the rate at which water passes by an impeller on the underside of the boat, registering the exact speed to the nearest $1/10$ mile per hour.

How to Return Your Plug to the Right Depth

NOTE the color when you hook a fish while using metered line, then let out to that color again. Most metered lines change color every 10 yards.

MARK your line with a waterproof pen when your plug is at the proper depth. Stop at the same mark when you let the plug out again.

COUNT the number of times the level-wind passes back and forth when letting out line. Use the same number of passes the next time.

Jerkbaits

A jerkbait imitates a large baitfish in distress, diving below the surface, then floating back up or darting erratically from side to side. The term *jerkbait* results from the sharp, jerky retrieve needed to give the plug its action. Jerkbaits have practically no action with a steady retrieve.

Nearly all jerkbaits are made of wood. They fall into two categories: high-buoyancy models, most of which have a metal tail to make them dive; and low-buoyancy

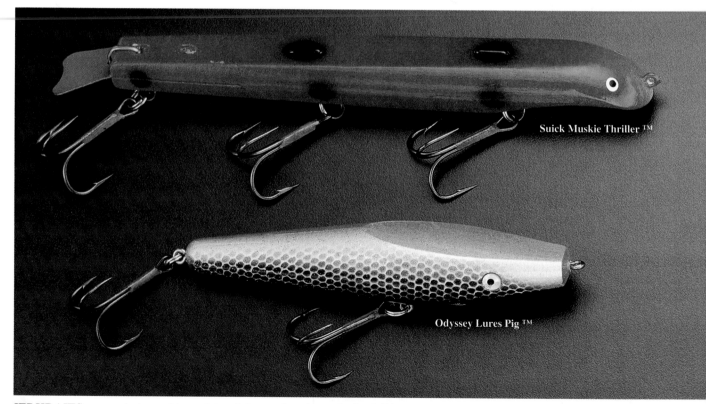

Suick Muskie Thriller ™

Odyssey Lures Pig ™

JERKBAITS are made in a wide variety of shapes, but the majority fall into two categories. They include *high-buoyancy* models, which have a fluke like metal tail and/or a grooved head to make them dive, and *low-buoyancy* models, which

Fishing with Jerkbaits

Many experts rate jerkbaits as the number-one lure for muskies and big pike. Although seldom used for other fish, jerkbaits sometimes take trophy-class walleyes and largemouth bass by accident.

A jerkbait appeals to big gamefish mainly because of its erratic action. As predator fish grow larger, they become lazier, and a baitfish moving erratically signals an easy meal.

You can rip a jerkbait through sparse weeds, retrieve it over weedtops or work it near a drop-off. After casting, reel up enough line so that the plug points straight toward you. Continue reeling while making sharp sweeps that can vary from 6 to 36 inches in length.

A high-buoyancy jerkbait rises quickly, so you must retrieve with closely spaced jerks to keep it from floating to the surface. Most fishermen find they can jerk more quickly with the rod tip pointing downward rather than sideways. When fished this way, these plugs dive rapidly, moving up and down more than side to side.

A low-buoyancy jerkbait will not dive as steeply. Short, sharp jerks will give it a side-to-side action;

models, which do not have tails. High-buoyancy models stop quickly after being jerked, then rise rapidly to the surface. Low-buoyancy models have more side-to-side action, glide forward after the jerk and rise to the surface more slowly.

Most jerkbaits dive from 2 to 4 feet, although some go as deep as 8 feet. Because the density of wood varies greatly, one jerkbait may dive or glide differently than another of the same model. Jerkbaits will catch fish throughout most of the open-water season. If the water temperature is below 60°F, use a low-buoyancy jerkbait and work it slowly. In warmer water, use either style of jerkbait and work it more rapidly.

When you give a jerkbait a sharp pull, it displaces a large volume of water as it darts ahead. Fish sense the sound and vibration, so they will strike jerkbaits in either clear or murky water.

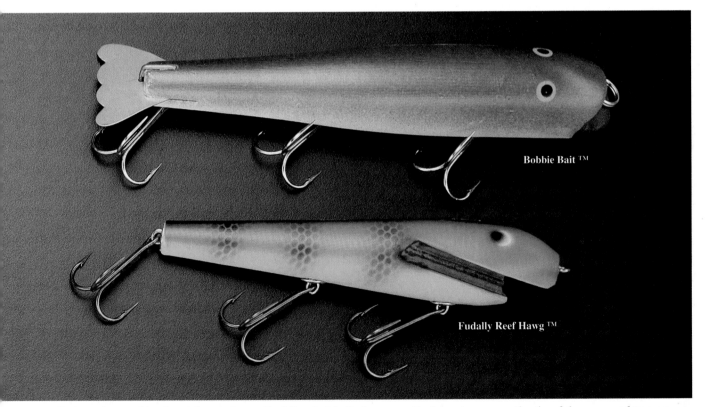

Bobbie Bait ™

Fudally Reef Hawg ™

usually have internal lead weights and no tails. Most jerkbaits have an attachment eye near the tip of the nose and two or three extra-strong treble hooks.

long, smooth jerks will give it an up-and-down, gliding action. Because the plug glides farther with each jerk and does not rise as quickly, the jerks can be more widely spaced. Ideally, the plug should follow a zigzag path 2 to 3 feet wide.

Experiment with the length and timing of your jerks to find the pattern that works best. Often a series of 2- to 3-inch tugs between longer jerks will trigger the fish to strike.

Casting is by far the most popular method for presenting jerkbaits, but trolling can also be effective. Motor along the edge of a weedbed while sweeping your rod sideways. Adjust your trolling speed to suit the action of the plug.

Some fishermen doctor their jerkbaits, especially high-buoyancy models, to make them run deeper, glide farther and float back to the surface more slowly. A doctored plug will often draw strikes from fish that ignore standard models. And you do not have to jerk as frantically to keep the plug from rising to the surface.

Setting the hook with a jerkbait is more difficult than with other plugs. Slack forms after each jerk,

and unless you reel up the loose line immediately, you will not be able to get enough leverage. Even if your line is tight, you may have difficulty. When a big pike or muskie clamps onto your jerkbait, only an extremely strong pull will break the fish's grip and move the plug far enough to sink the hooks.

To set the hook this hard, you need a very stiff rod. Jerkbaits may weigh as much as 4 ounces, so a stiff rod is also necessary for casting and retrieving them properly. A rod with a long handle provides extra leverage for casting and setting the hook.

Most fishermen use 30- to 50-pound low-stretch line on a sturdy, free-spool reel. Dacron or braided superline will not stretch and cause you to lose hook-setting power. If your jerkbait comes with a leader attached, additional snaps or leaders are unnecessary. If it does not have a leader, attach a solid-wire or multi-strand wire leader of at least 45-pound test.

A common mistake in fishing with jerkbaits is horsing the fish after you set the hook. With a stiff rod and heavy, nonstretch line, you can easily rip the hook loose unless you play the fish carefully.

How to Doctor a Jerkbait

DETERMINE the proper weight distribution by attaching sinkers to the belly with double-faced tape.

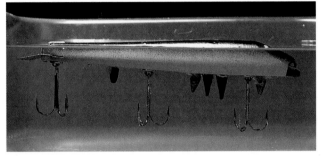

TEST the flotation of your plug after attaching the sinkers by placing it in a tub of water. Continue taping sinkers in different positions until the plug floats level with its back barely out of the water.

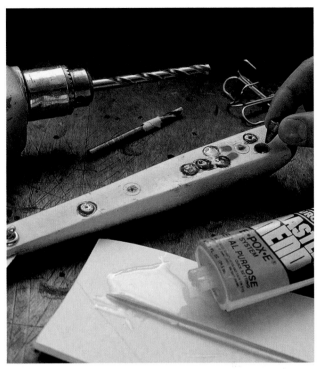

DRILL holes exactly where the sinkers were attached. If using cone sinkers, drill a small hole for the nose, then drill out the top of the hole for the base. Partially fill the holes with epoxy, seat the sinkers, then seal.

Tips for Fishing with Jerkbaits

BEND the metal tail down slightly to make the plug dive more sharply. Bend one side of the tail down to make the plug veer more to that side.

PLACE a strip of fluorescent tape on the back of your jerkbait. The tape helps you see the plug in the water so you can control its action.

STORE jerkbaits and other large lures by pushing the hooks into the lip of a Styrofoam® cooler. The lures dry quickly and do not snag your net.

Soft Plastics

Soft Plastics

Fishermen have used soft-bodied lures since 1860, when the first rubber worm was patented. But most of the early lures lacked the lifelike action of modern soft plastics because the material was relatively hard by today's standards.

In 1949, an Ohio luremaker began molding plastic worms from a new synthetic material, polyvinyl chloride resin. Bass fishermen who tested these lures soon reported fantastic results. Because the worms were so soft, they flexed with each twitch of the line, resulting in an irresistible action.

The popularity of soft plastics has skyrocketed since those early years. Most tackle stores now offer a wide selection of soft plastic worms, grubs, crayfish, shrimp, frogs, snakes, lizards, salamanders, salmon eggs and insect imitations. Today, fishermen use soft plastic lures for virtually all species of gamefish.

Soft plastics offer several major advantages over hard-bodied lures. A hard-bodied artificial does not have a texture like real food, so fish may immediately recognize it as a fake and eject it. If you do not set the hook instantly, you will probably miss the fish. But a soft plastic has a lifelike texture, so fish will mouth it an instant longer, giving you extra time to set the hook.

Many soft plastics can be rigged with the hook point buried inside where it cannot catch on obstructions. This way, a soft plastic can be retrieved through dense weeds or brush, or over rocks and logs with practically no chance of snagging. Yet the point will penetrate the soft material when you set the hook.

Another attribute of soft plastics is their ability to absorb scents. You can treat soft plastics with bottled fish attractants or buy them with scents molded in. Scents quickly wash off hard-bodied lures, but soft plastic holds scent much longer.

Often, soft plastics look almost exactly like natural fish foods. Legs, feelers and even minute details like scales add to the realistic appearance. Many have translucent bodies that allow light to pass through, much as it passes through common foods like baitfish, worms, shrimp and insect larvae.

Modern soft plastics vary in hardness from almost jellylike to relatively firm. The softer lures look and feel more natural to fish. But the harder ones are more durable and stay on the hook better, especially when fished in snaggy cover. Most manufacturers use a plastic between these extremes.

To cast the smallest soft plastic lures, you will need light spinning tackle, light line, sinkers or a casting bubble. Or you can use fly tackle. To cast soft plastics less than 6 inches long, light spinning tackle and 4- to 8-pound mono usually work best. For larger lures with exposed hooks, most fishermen prefer spinning or baitcasting tackle with lines from 8- to 15-pound test. For larger soft plastic lures with hooks buried in the plastic, use baitcasting tackle with lines from 12- to 25-pound test.

Some manufacturers make powerful rods, called *worm rods,* specifically for driving the hook point through a soft plastic lure and into a fish's jaw. When working soft plastics through weeds or brush, use abrasion-resistant line.

BASIC SOFT PLASTIC LURES include worms, grubs, tubes, craws, lizards, soft stickbaits, minnows and soft plastic surface baits.

Soft Plastic Lures

Soft plastic lures entice strikes with their tantalizing action and can be rigged weedless to go into dense cover without snagging. Rigged Texas-style (p. 67), soft plastics work better than any other lure for probing thick weeds, brush or flooded timber. And if the bait does become snagged, you can break it off and tie on a new one for only a few pennies.

Color can be an important consideration in choosing soft plastics. Soft plastic baits come in a staggering variety of colors. Darker and more natural colors seem to work best in clear to slightly stained water, where fish have better visibility. When fishing plastics on or near the surface in low light periods, dark-colored plastics offer a better silhouette for the fish to see. Generally, brighter colors, metal-flake and fire-tail baits will work better in stained or dirty water and will often draw more strikes than baits in darker colors.

The shape of the tail can also be an important consideration when selecting a bait. Curly-tails wiggle enticingly when retrieved and are an excellent choice in current. Curly-tails and skirted-tails sink more slowly than other tails. Paddle-tails have a good swimming action when fished with a jigging retrieve.

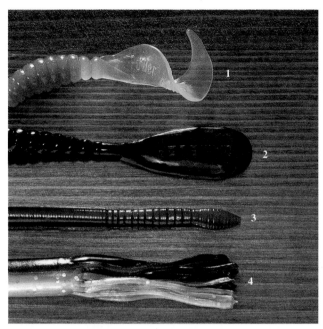

PRE-RIGGED worms are manufactured with hooks embedded in the bait. The hooks are usually exposed and may snag easily if the hooks don't come with weed-guards. Some are rigged with a type of spinner to add vibrations to the bait.

TAIL SHAPE determines the action of a soft plastic lure. Popular tail designs include (1) curly-tail or twister tail, which are used on worms, grubs and lizards, (2) paddle-tail or flap-tail for minnows and worms, (3) straight-tail for worms and soft stickbaits, and (4) skirted-tail, usually found on tube baits or grubs.

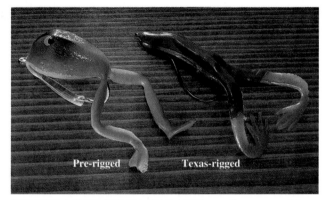

Pre-rigged   Texas-rigged

SOFT PLASTIC SURFACE BAITS usually come with the hooks built into the bait. On some, the body can be replaced if the plastic is torn up, while others, it can't. Some baits do not come with hooks and are usually fished Texas-style.

Flap-tails on minnow plastics give off a good vibration and have an enticing action. Straight-tails have less action than other types. They work best for tying threaded multiple-hook rigs (p. 67).

Selecting the size of the soft plastic not only depends on the species of fish, but on the time of year and the water clarity. Small baits usually work best in spring, before the water warms. Larger soft plastics are a better choice in summer, when fish become more active. Small plastics are generally best in clear water; larger baits in murky water.

Buoyancy can also be a consideration. A bait that rides above bottom is easily visible to fish and less prone to snagging. And you need the buoyancy when floating a soft plastic bait on the surface. Most plastics will float, but many are not buoyant enough to float when rigged with a hook. When flotation is important, use a soft plastic made from highly buoyant material or one with air pockets molded in.

A few worms come pre-rigged with a monofilament hook harness threaded into the body. This type of rigging works well when fish are striking short. But pre-rigged worms snag easily and generally lack the action of other worms. The majority of soft plastic surface baits are made with the hooks built into the lure in a manner that makes them weedless. Some do not come pre-rigged and are usually fished Texas-rigged.

Most soft plastics come without hooks, so you can rig them to suit your fishing situation. When rigging Texas-style, choose a hook with a long, sharp point that will easily penetrate the plastic. The shaft must be bent at the proper angle for good penetration, and it should have barbs or sharp bends to keep the plastic bait from sliding back when you set the hook. Also, consider the gap of the hook when fishing a particular soft plastic. Make sure that the gap will penetrate the bait and still have enough room to hook the fish. With a Carolina rig (p. 67), use a plain, straight-shank hook, a hook with a light wire weedguard or the same type of hook used for Texas-style rigging.

Fishing with Soft Plastics

A hungry largemouth bass finds it difficult to resist a soft plastic bait squirming seductively through its underwater hideout. Plastic baits appeal most strongly to largemouth bass, but also work very well for small-mouth and spotted bass, white bass, stripers, sunfish, northern pike, muskie, walleyes and even brown trout.

Plastics come in a variety of sizes. Some basic guidelines include: for panfish, usually less than 2 inches long; for smallmouth and spotted bass, white bass, walleyes and brown trout, 3 to 6 inches; for most largemouth bass and stripers, 4 to 8 inches; and for northern pike, muskie and big largemouths, 9 to 13 inches.

For bass and panfish, plastics work best starting when the water temperature reaches 60°F in spring and continuing until the temperature drops below 60°F in fall. Soft plastics remain effective at cooler temperatures for most other species.

Fishing with most plastics bears many similarities to fishing with jigs. Fish usually grab a bait as it sinks, so you need a sensitive touch to detect a strike. You must keep your line taut as the bait drops, or strikes will go unnoticed.

The way you rig your soft plastic depends on the fishing situation. For fishing in weeds, brush, timber or other dense cover, rig your bait Texas-style. Because the hook point is buried inside the plastic, you can retrieve the bait over obstructions without snagging.

You can also rig your bait on a weedless single hook when fishing in heavy cover. Because the point is exposed, you can set the hook more easily. But baits rigged this way catch more debris than those rigged Texas-style.

When snags are not a problem, thread your soft plastic on a jig head with a barbed collar, or use a multiple-hook rig. The exposed hooks will improve your hooking percentage.

The Carolina rig (opposite page) is good for deep-water fishing. The swivel prevents the line from twisting and keeps the sinker from sliding down the line.

When rigging Texas- or Carolina-style, use a hook from size #2 to 1/0 with a 4-inch bait; 1/0 to 3/0 with a 6-inch bait; 4/0 or 5/0 with an 8-inch bait; and 5/0 or 6/0 with a 10- to 13-inch bait.

A common mistake in rigging soft plastics Texas-style is to use too much weight. A bait slithering slowly draws more strikes than one sinking rapidly. With a standard 6-inch worm or other similar-size bait, a 1/8-ounce sinker is usually adequate at depths of 10 feet or less. Seldom will you need a sinker weighing more than 1/4 ounce. When fishing with a Carolina rig in deep water, use a sinker of 1/2 ounce or more.

Inexperienced worm or other plastic bait fishermen often use rods that are too soft, so they fail to set the hook hard enough. To drive the hook point through the plastic and into a fish's jaw, use a stiff rod. When you detect a strike, lower the rod tip and reel up the slack rapidly, then set the hook as hard as you can. Expert fishermen often set the hook two or three times to make sure it sinks in.

How to Rig a Soft Plastic Texas-style

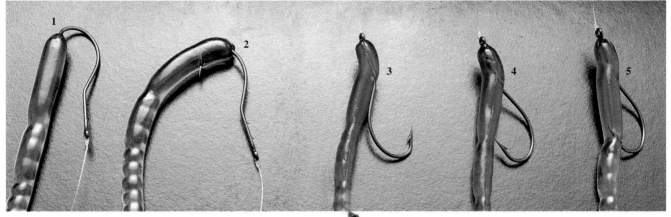

TEXAS-RIG a plastic worm or other soft bait by (1) inserting the point of the hook into the head end. (2) Push the hook about ½ inch into the head, then out the side. (3) Continue threading the hook through the worm, leaving only the eye protruding. (4) Twist the hook one-half turn. (5) Push the hook into the bait until the point almost penetrates the opposite side, and pull the head of the bait over the hook eye. The rigged soft plastic should hang straight with no kinks or twists.

How to Tie a Multiple-hook Rig

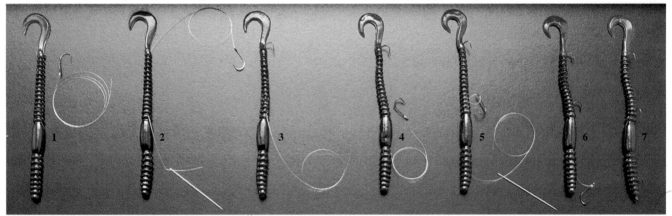

TIE (1) a length of 6-pound mono to a #6 hook. (2) With a needle, thread the line into the tail and out the middle of a 6-inch worm. (3) Pull the line to draw the hook into the worm. (4) Tie on another hook using a nail knot (p. 13). (5) Thread the line into the same hole, then out a hook's length behind the head. (6) Pull the middle hook into the worm, then nail-knot a third hook to the mono; trim. (7) Push the hook, eye first, into the hole, then up to the tip of the head. The mono inside the worm should be taut, but not tight enough to kink the worm.

Other Rigging Methods

MAKE a Carolina rig by threading a buoyant soft plastic onto a barbed-shank hook, leaving the point exposed. Or use a worm hook and bury the point. Tie the hook to an 18- to 36-inch leader attached to a slip-sinker rig.

THREAD a worm or other plastic onto a lead jig head with a barbed collar. Push firmly to snug the bait against the jig head so there is no gap. Mushroom-head jigs work especially well for this type of rigging.

HOP a Texas-rigged worm through timber, brush or dense weeds. If the worm catches on an obstruction, twitch the rod to free it. To prevent the sinker from sliding away from the worm, peg the sinker in place by wedging a piece of toothpick into the hole and breaking it off.

SKIP a plastic bait under a dock or other overhanging cover to reach bass hiding in the shade. Keep your rod tip low, then snap your wrist sharply. Spinning rods work best for this presentation.

FLIP a Texas-rigged plastic so it lands alongside a tree trunk or in any hard-to-reach spot. Keep your line taut as the bait sinks and be ready to set the hook at any sign of a twitch or pause. When using this technique, most fishermen prefer a stiff rod about 7½ feet long.

RETRIEVE a 2- to 3-inch plastic worm along the edge of submerged weeds or over weedtops to catch sunfish. Use a #6 or #8 hook and leave the point exposed. If the fish are striking short, use a multiple-hook rig with two #8 hooks.

RIG a plastic lizard on a jig head when fishing over weed-tops or along a weedline. If the open hook catches on vegetation, jerk sharply to free it. Use a jig head with a double-barbed collar to prevent the lizard from slipping back when you jerk.

CRAWL an unweighted plastic worm over pads or other surface vegetation. Retrieve with twitches and pauses. Use a highly buoyant worm and a small hook for maximum flotation. You may need lighter-than-normal line to cast the nearly weightless rig.

Tips for Fishing with Soft Plastics

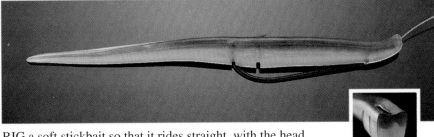

RIG a soft stickbait so that it rides straight, with the head angled upward. The lighter the cover, the more you can push the hook point through the plastic without the risk of fouling. The point is protected by the bait's concave back (inset of cross section); in some brands, there is a slot to protect the hook point from fouling.

BOIL warped baits for about 30 seconds. Lay them on their back to dry, making sure they're straight. Boiling them too long softens them too much.

AVOID storing soft plastics with painted lures, plastic hook or swivel boxes or plastics of different colors. The resin eats the paint or plastic, and the colors bleed.

Jigs & Jigging Lures

Jigs & Jigging Lures

Many expert fishermen consider jigs and jigging lures the most consistently productive of all artificial lures. They work for a wide variety of species under almost any conditions.

A jig is simply a piece of lead with a hook molded into it. A dressing of hair, feathers, tinsel or soft plastic generally conceals the hook. Other types of jigging lures include the jigging spoon, a very thick metal spoon; the vibrating blade, a thin metal minnow imitation; and the tailspin, a lead-bodied lure with a spinner at the rear.

Jigs and jigging lures can be fished slowly, so they work especially well in cold water. Low water temperature reduces the metabolic rate of fish, making them reluctant to chase fast-moving lures. But the slow jigging action will often tempt a strike. The rapid sink rate of most jigs and jigging lures makes them an excellent choice for reaching bottom in current or for fishing in deep water. Lake trout anglers, for example, regularly use these lures at depths of up to 100 feet with no extra weight added to the line. But jigs and jigging lures can also be effective in water only a few feet deep.

Most jigs and jigging lures have compact bodies, so they are ideal for casting into the wind or for casting long distances. The extra distance helps you take fish in clear water or in other situations where they are easily spooked.

Despite the effectiveness of jigs and jigging lures, many anglers have difficulty catching fish with them. The main problem is detecting the strike. Fish seldom slam these lures as they do a crankbait or surface lure. Instead, they inhale the lure gently, usually as it settles toward bottom. If you are not alert or do not have a taut line as the lure sinks, you will not notice the strike.

Because strikes are often light, jigs and jigging lures should be fished with sensitive tackle. Most experts prefer a relatively stiff graphite rod, with just enough flexibility in the tip to cast the lure.

Ultralight to medium-power spinning or light baitcasting outfits work well in most cases. But heavier tackle is needed to handle lures over 3/4 ounce or to horse fish from heavy cover.

Use the lightest line practical for the species and fishing conditions. If your line is too heavy, the lure will sink too slowly and will not stay at the desired depth when retrieved. Also, strikes will be more difficult to detect.

With ordinary monofilament, the twitch signaling a strike is hard to see. To detect strikes more easily, use fluorescent monofilament. Many jig fishermen wear polarized sunglasses to improve line visibility even more.

When selecting jigs and jigging lures, the main consideration is weight. Your selection must be a compromise based on the type of fish, water depth, current speed and wind velocity.

For panfish, most anglers prefer lures of no more than 1/8 ounce. Some panfish jigs, called *micro jigs,* weigh as little as 1/80 ounce. For mid-sized gamefish like walleyes and bass, 1/4- to 1½-ounce lures normally work best. For larger gamefish, lures of 1 ounce or more are usually most productive.

The lure must be heavy enough to reach the desired depth, but not so heavy that it sinks too fast. Fish usually prefer a slowly falling lure to one plummeting toward bottom. As a general rule, allow 1/8 ounce for every 10 feet of water. For example, a lure of at least 1/4 ounce would be needed to reach bottom in water 20 feet deep.

In slow current, however, the same 1/4-ounce lure would only reach a depth of about 15 feet. As the current becomes faster, the weight of lure needed to reach bottom increases. Wind affects your lure choice much the same way as current. The wind pushes your boat across the surface, increasing water resistance on the line and lure. This makes it more difficult for the lure to reach the desired depth and stay there.

Jigs

The way a jig performs depends not only on its weight, but also on its head design, the type of dressing and the hook style.

HEAD DESIGN. The head shape and the position of the hook eye affect a jig's sink rate, action and resistance to snagging or tangling in weeds. Following are the most popular head designs:

Ball — This common, fast-sinking head works well in most situations. But the hook eye, which is on top, tends to catch weeds.

Keel — Flattened vertically, this thin head slices through the water with little resistance and sinks rapidly. It is ideal for fast current or deep water.

Bullet — Another fast-sinking design, the bullet head cuts easily through current. Because it does not settle as rapidly as a keel head when jigged, it snags less and is usually more appealing to fish.

Slider — A slider head is flattened horizontally, so it sinks slowly and glides through the water. It is most effective in shallow water and for suspended fish.

Mushroom — This head was designed for use with soft plastic tails. The plastic can be snugged up flush to the head, and a double barb on the collar keeps it from sliding back. This makes it a good choice for ripping through weeds.

Banana — Because the hook eye is far forward on this head, the tail points up when you lower the lure and down when you raise it. The sharp kicking action makes this head ideal for vertical jigging.

Stand-up — This head is designed so that the tail and hook stand up when the jig rests on bottom. The high-riding hook makes the jig fairly snag-resistant.

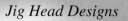

Jig Head Designs

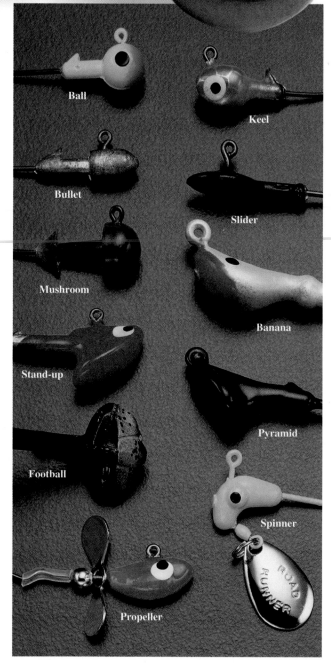

Ball

Keel

Bullet

Slider

Mushroom

Banana

Stand-up

Pyramid

Football

Spinner

Propeller

Pyramid — The hook eye is at the front tip of the tapered head, so weeds tend to slide over the head instead of catching on the eye.

Football — This oblong-shaped head is designed to stand up when at rest or when being dragged across the bottom. The hook eye is on top of the jig.

Other head styles — Others have a spinner blade or propeller for extra flash and sound.

DRESSING. The type of dressing affects the sink rate and action of a jig. Most jigs come with some type of natural or synthetic dressing. Plain jig heads are used only in combination with live bait. Following are the most popular jig dressings:

Hair — Natural hair gives a jig an attractive pulsing action. And hair is durable, enabling you to catch many fish on the same jig. Bucktail hair works especially well. It holds its shape and its natural buoyancy slows the sink rate, making the action more tantalizing. Other popular types of hair include calf tail, squirrel tail and rabbit.

Feathers — Airy feathers such as marabou have an enticing, breathing action unlike that of any other material. Stiffer feathers are used as tails or hackle collars. But feathers lack the durability of hair.

Soft plastic — These dressings feel like real food, so a fish may mouth the jig longer before recognizing it as a fake. This extra instant improves your chances of setting the hook. And like bucktail, soft plastic slows a jig's sink rate.

Curly-tailed soft plastics wiggle enticingly. Other soft plastics imitate natural foods like minnows, crayfish and grubs.

Soft plastic tails are less durable than most other dressings. They tear after catching a few fish, and a pike, muskie or walleye can easily bite them off.

Silicone — Silicone tails have a billowing action, and their buoyancy causes the jig to sink slowly. This dressing is very durable. Soft plastic trailers or dressings are often combined with silicone on a single jig.

Other dressings — Tinsel and Mylar® tails are extremely durable and reflect light well. Imitation-hair tails made of nylon or other synthetics are tough, but mat easily and lack the action of real hair.

Fishermen sometimes combine the regular jig dressings with pork rind trailers, minnows or a wide variety of other live baits.

HOOK STYLE. How well a hook penetrates and holds a fish and how easily it unsnags depend mainly on its thickness. Most jigs come with fine-wire Aberdeen hooks that penetrate easily. When

Jig Dressings

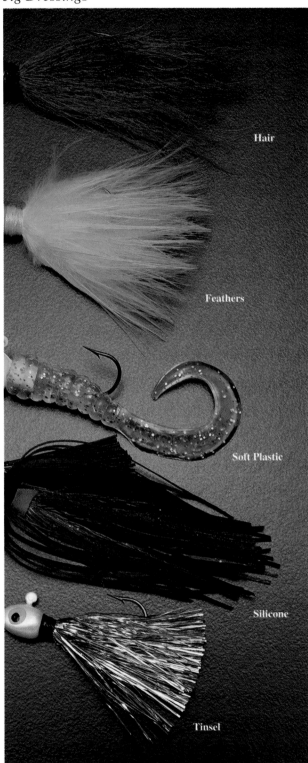

snagged, they can often be straightened with a direct pull on the line. Heavier O'Shaughnessy-style hooks work better for tough-jawed fish and for horsing fish out of dense cover.

Some hooks have a *brushguard* made of nylon bristles, a Y-shaped plastic strip or a piece of heavy mono.

Fishing with Jigs

With the right jig and the right presentation, you can catch everything from quarter-pound sunfish to 40-pound lake trout.

The most common way to fish a jig is to cast to a likely spot, then retrieve in short hops along bottom. Another effective method is to jig vertically in tight spots or while drifting with the wind or current. When fish are suspended, you can count your jig down to different depths until you find the most productive level.

You can also troll with jigs. Slow trolling along structure will take a wide variety of fish, including walleyes, northern pike and largemouth and small-mouth bass. As you move along, twitch your rod tip to hop the jig over the bottom. Trolling steadily in midwater will catch fish like white bass, stripers and crappies. When using this method, add a soft plastic curlytail to your jig to improve its action.

Many anglers believe jigs are effective only on a clean bottom because they snag easily in brush and foul in weeds. But a light jig works well when hopped over weed or brushtops. With a little practice, you can keep it dancing inches above the cover.

Tipping your jig with live bait like minnows, worms, leeches or insect larvae will often improve your results. But you may have to use a stinger hook (p. 81) to catch short strikers.

Catching fish on jigs requires a high level of concentration, a fine-tuned sense of feel and quick reflexes. If you fail to pay constant attention, if you are not accustomed to recognizing subtle strikes or if you do not set the hook immediately, chances are you will go home with an empty stringer.

You can improve your jig-fishing skills by following these guidelines:

• Keep your line taut at all times, especially as the jig sinks. But the line should not be so tight that it interferes with the action of the jig.

• Stay alert for any twitch or sideways movement of the line.

• Watch your line carefully to make sure the jig sinks normally after the cast and when jigging. If it stops sinking unexpectedly, a fish has probably grabbed it.

• Set the hook at the slightest indication of a strike. Do not hesitate; a fish can pick up the jig and expel it in an instant.

Always tie your jig directly to the line, without snaps, swivels or other connectors. A loop knot like the Duncan loop (p. 12) will allow the jig to swing freely, maximizing its action. When fishing for northern pike, pickerel or muskies, attach a wire leader to your jig using a twist-melt connection or haywire twist (p. 14).

Most serious jig fishermen carry a jig box stocked with a wide variety of heads and dressings for different species and situations. Often, a head weighing $1/8$ ounce more or less than the one you are using can make a big difference.

Basic Bottom-bouncing Technique

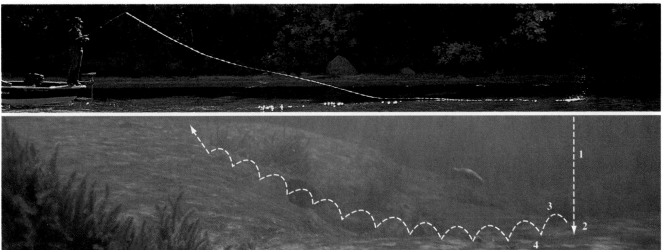

CAST your jig past the fish zone, then (1) pay out line as the jig sinks. When the jig hits bottom, (2) your line will go slack. Tighten your line slightly, then (3) twitch the rod tip to make the jig hop forward. As the jig sinks, (4) lower the rod tip slowly to keep the line taut. Keeping a taut line at this point is the key to success with this technique. Continue to hop the jig this way until you can no longer maintain contact with bottom.

REEL a spinner-type jig steadily over logs or brush in shallow water. The resistance of the blade reduces the sink rate, so you can retrieve slowly without snagging. This technique is best for bass and crappies.

TIP a plain, fluorescent-colored jig head with a minnow, leech or piece of nightcrawler when fish refuse to strike dressed jigs. The fluorescent head draws attention, and the plain hook will not hide the bait.

HOP a stand-up jig over a snaggy bottom. The hook seldom hangs up because the jig usually comes to rest with the tail pointing upward. And the upright tail is easy for fish to see.

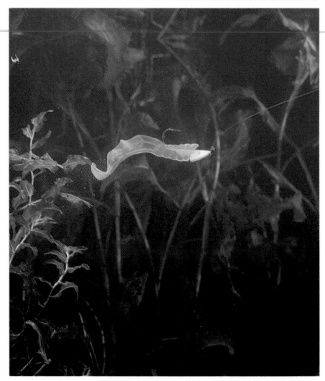

RIP a pyramid or mushroom jig through sparse weeds or along the edges of thicker patches. When the jig hits weeds, jerk your rod sharply with a snap of the wrist to tear it loose. A short, stout rod works best.

SUSPEND a micro jig from a pencil float to fish over brush or weeds. Twitch the float so the jig rises, then settles back to the cover. Set the hook when the float tips up. This method works especially well for crappies.

FLIP a brushguard jig alongside a tree or into a tight pocket in weeds or brush. Flippin' enables you to fish targets quickly and accurately. A banana-head jig dressed with a pork strip is ideal for this technique.

Jig Sink Rate (sink rate measured in feet per second)

HEAD STYLE		JIG WEIGHT					
		1/8 ounce	1/4 ounce	3/8 ounce	1/2 ounce	3/4 ounce	1 ounce
	Ball	2.4	3.5	4.4	5.2	6.1	6.4
	Keel	—	3.2	4.1	4.6	5.5	6.0
	Bullet	2.2	3.3	4.0	4.6	5.5	6.0
	Slider	1.7	2.0	1.5*	—	—	—
	Mushroom	2.2	3.3	3.9	4.4	—	—
	Banana	—	2.9	3.3	3.7	4.4	4.9
	Stand-up	—	3.3	3.9	4.4	—	—
	Pyramid	2.3	3.4	4.0	4.6	—	—

NOTES: All sink rates were measured with jig heads tied to a 6~pound test line • Only commonly available weights were tested • All jig heads were tested without dressing. Dressed jigs normally sink 5 to 10% slower.

*Sink rate slower than expected due to flattened jig head trapping an air bubble.

How to Rig Soft Plastic Dressings

SELECT a (1) jig head with large barbs on the collar. The barbs keep the tail from sliding back each time you attempt to set the hook. To rig a (2) curly-tail grub, center the hook on the front of the body and push it through so that only the bend and point protrude. Insert the hook into a (3) shad and out through the midline of the back. Be sure the hook penetrates the back, not the belly. Rig a (4) crayfish on a slider head by pushing the hook through the body from the bottom up. The point should

Tips for Using Jigs

ANCHOR a soft plastic tail to the jig head to keep the tail from sliding back. Apply a drop of superglue to the collar, then push the tail forward. Let the glue dry before using the jig.

MOLD your own jigs using tin rather than lead. A tin jig sinks more slowly than a lead jig of the same size and shape. And the tin has a permanent shine that appeals to many gamefish.

SHORTEN your jig tail to improve your hooking percentage when fish are striking short. A jig with a shortened tail appears smaller and often draws more strikes.

CAST downstream when fishing in a river with a snaggy bottom. If your jig hangs up, allow your line to drift with the current. Continue feeding line until the belly is 20 to 30 feet below the spot where you are snagged. Point your rod tip at the

come out just behind the head. Press the tail over the hook eye until the eye comes through. Thread on a (5) Sassy Shiner™ so that the hook protrudes between the dorsal fins. The fins help keep the hook from fouling, making the lure semi-weedless. Position a (6) paddle-tail grub with the flat part of the tail turned horizontally. This way, the grub tail pumps up and down when you jig the lure.

TIE a #10 or 12 treble hook, or stinger, to the bend of your jig hook to catch short-striking fish. Pierce the head of a minnow with the jig hook; the tail with one prong of the stinger.

CHOOSE jigs with fine-wire hooks when fishing around flooded trees or stumps. The hook will straighten enough so you can free it from a snag, and you can easily bend it back.

BITE a piece from the tail of a soft plastic shad or shiner to improve its action. Reducing the thickness of the tail makes it more flexible, increasing the amount of side-to-side wiggle.

snag, then pull sharply with a long, sweeping motion. Water resistance against the belly of the line enables you to exert a downstream tug, which usually frees the jig.

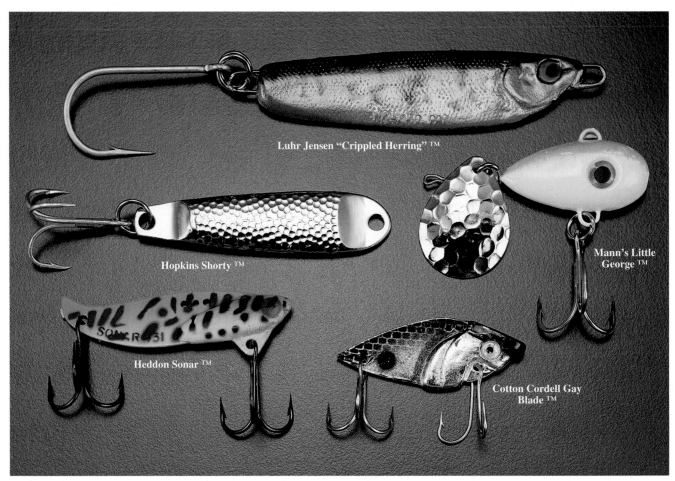

JIGGING LURES include jigging spoons, vibrating blades and tailspins.

Luhr Jensen "Crippled Herring" ™

Hopkins Shorty ™

Mann's Little George ™

Heddon Sonar ™

Cotton Cordell Gay Blade ™

Jigging Lures

Jigging lures, unlike most jigs, have some type of built-in action. All jigging lures can be fished with a jigging motion, and some also work well with a straight retrieve. Jigging lures are divided into the following categories:

JIGGING SPOONS. These lures resemble spoons used for casting or trolling, but are generally thicker and flatter. Most are made of lead, chromed brass or stainless steel. Because jigging spoons have treble hooks, they hang up more often than jigs. But they unsnag easily, so they are ideal for fishing in timber and brush.

Long, thin jigging spoons are used mainly for vertical jigging, but also work for casting. Shorter, wider spoons, called *slab spoons,* resemble small shad. Their compact shape

82

makes them effective for distance casting to schools of gamefish pursuing shad on or near the surface.

VIBRATING BLADES. These lures have a lead head, a thin steel tail, and treble hooks at each end. A series of line-attachment holes enables you to change the balance and action. Vibrating blades can be used for vertical jigging, casting or trolling.

TAILSPINS. The thick lead body has a wire at the rear that serves as a shaft for a spinner blade. Most tailspins have one treble hook attached to the bottom, but some have another treble behind the spinner blade. The attachment eye is at the top. Tailspins are excellent for vertical jigging and casting to surface-schooling fish.

How the Action of Jigging Lures Differs

JIGGING SPOONS flash and flutter erratically when allowed to sink on a slack line. They tip slightly from side to side when retrieved. But jigging spoons generally lack the typical wobbling action associated with most other types of spoons.

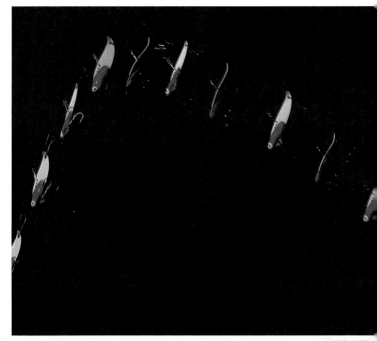

VIBRATING BLADES wiggle rapidly when pulled through the water but have no action as they sink. Attaching the line farther to the rear increases the wiggle.

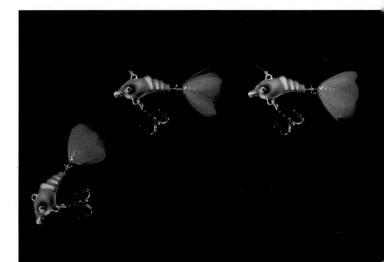

TAILSPINS have a spinner blade that turns when the lure is pulled forward and helicopters when the lure is allowed to sink. Tailspins lack the fluttering or wiggling action of other jigging lures, but the constant rotation of the blade provides more flash.

Fishing with Jigging Spoons

When fish are buried in heavy cover or holding along vertical structure, no other lure works as well as a jigging spoon. Its density causes it to sink quickly, so you can lower it into tight spots where other lures would be difficult to present.

You can jig a spoon vertically in a small opening in a stand of flooded timber, over a deep brush pile or alongside a bridge piling or sheer cliff. Or you can jig it vertically while drifting with the wind or current. You can also cast a jigging spoon and retrieve it along bottom, as you would a jig.

A jigging spoon has an attractive fluttering action when it sinks. But if you keep the line too tight, the spoon will not flutter. As the spoon sinks, maintain less tension than you would with a jig.

Jigging spoons are most effective when the water is cool or cold and fish hold tight to cover, refusing fast-moving lures. Under these conditions, you must work the lure slowly and present it within inches of the fish.

A fish strikes a jigging spoon much the same way it strikes a jig. Set the hook at any tap, or if the line moves sideways or fails to drop as expected.

Fishermen use spoons weighing from 1/8 to 1/4 ounce for crappies and white bass; 1/4 to 1 ounce for large-mouth, smallmouth and spotted bass; and 1 to 2 1/2 ounces for lake trout and stripers.

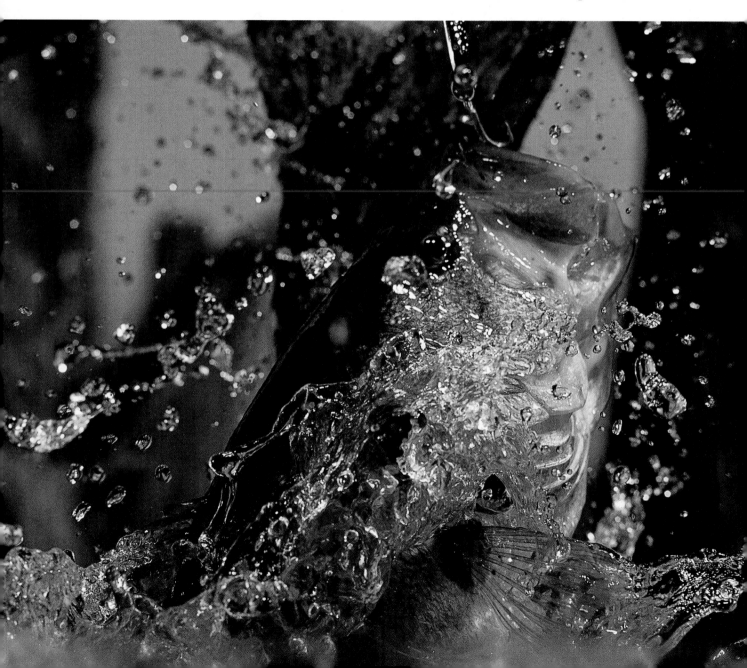

Tips for Using Jigging Spoons

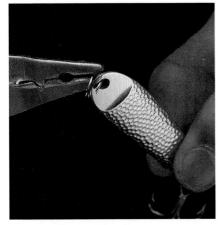

ATTACH a split-ring to the eye using a split-ring pliers. Tying directly to the eye restricts the action, and the sharp edge will fray your line.

CAST a slab spoon to a surface school of white bass, stripers or largemouths. Circling gulls often pinpoint a school. Start your retrieve as soon as the spoon hits the water, and hold your rod tip high to keep the lure from sinking. A rapid retrieve usually draws more strikes than a slow one.

WORK a jigging spoon along the shady side of a standing tree or other vertical cover. Lower the spoon a few feet, then jig it at that depth for several seconds. Continue lowering and jigging until you reach bottom.

SET the hook with a sharp upward motion when using a jigging spoon on monofilament line in deep water. Monofilament stretches easily so a strong hook set is needed to hook the fish.

BEND a jigging spoon to give it the best action for your type of fishing. A straight body or slight bend is adequate for vertical jigging. A more pronounced bend produces a wider wobble and works better for casting.

FREE a snagged spoon by raising your rod gently until the line is taut. Do not pull hard or the hook will sink in deeper. Drop the rod tip rapidly; the impact of the heavy spoon falling will usually dislodge the hook.

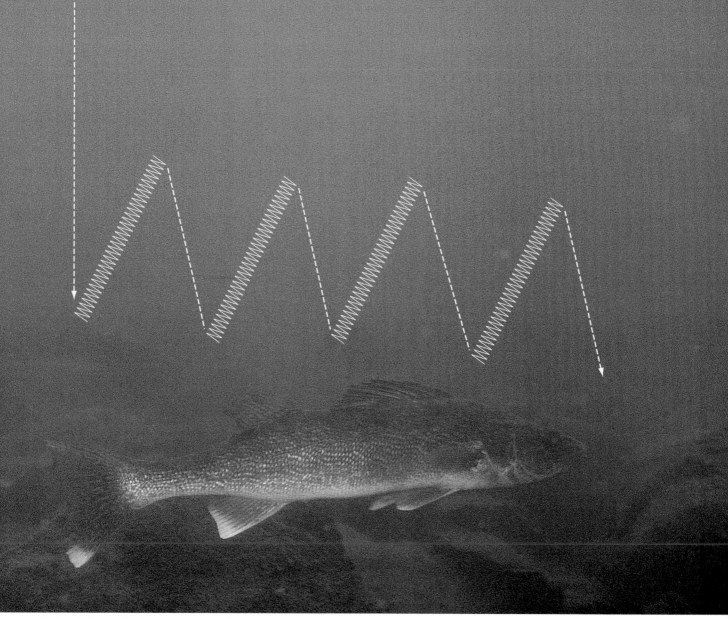

JIG a blade vertically by sweeping your rod upward to make the lure vibrate. Experiment with sweeps ranging from 1 to 4 feet, always keeping the line taut while the lure sinks. Fish almost always strike on the drop.

Fishing with Vibrating Blades

A vibrating blade attracts gamefish with its intense wiggling action. Because fish can detect vibrating blades with their lateral-line sense as well as with their sense of sight, the lures work well even in turbid water.

Fishermen use blades weighing from 1/8 to 1/4 ounce for white bass and crappies; from 1/4 to 1/2 ounce for walleyes, largemouths and smallmouths; and from 1/2 to 1 ounce for stripers and lake trout.

You can fish a vibrating blade by jigging vertically, casting or trolling. Vertical jigging generally works best over a fairly clean bottom. Because a blade

lacks the density of a jigging spoon, it is not as easy to free should it become snagged.

When casting or "trolling" with a vibrating blade, keep the lure moving steadily, much as you would with a crankbait. The fast sink rate of a blade enables you to reach deeper water than you could with most crankbaits. You can also hop a vibrating blade across bottom. The hopping retrieve is much like the bottom-bouncing technique described on page 77, but you must use longer upward sweeps to make the blade vibrate.

Vibrating blades have two or three holes along the back for attaching your line. How much the lure wiggles and the depth at which it runs depend on where you attach the line. Experiment with different attachment holes to determine the one that works best for your fishing situation.

Tips for Using Vibrating Blades

CONNECT a blade with a plain snap instead of a snap-swivel. The hooks swing up when the lure sinks and may foul on a longer swivel.

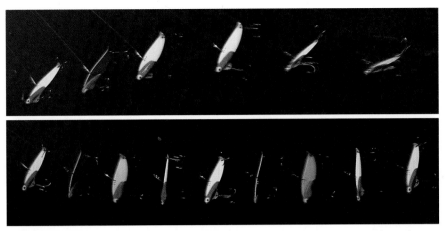

CLIP your line to the front attachment hole of a vibrating blade to produce the tightest vibration and make the lure run deepest on the retrieve (top). Connect the line to the rear hole to produce the widest wobble and make the lure run shallowest (bottom).

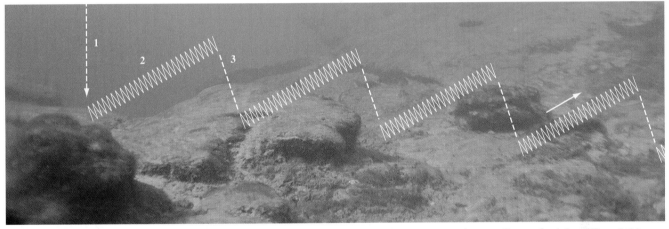

HOP a vibrating blade along bottom by first casting beyond the fish zone, then (1) paying out line as it sinks. When it hits bottom, (2) sweep your rod upward fast enough to make the blade vibrate. To detect strikes, (3) keep your line taut as the lure sinks. Continue hopping the blade, using longer sweeps than you would with a jig.

LOCATE lake trout in deep water with a vibrating blade. After jigging vertically on bottom, reel the lure rapidly upward. Stop to jig every 10 to 20 feet. Lakers often follow the lure, striking near the surface.

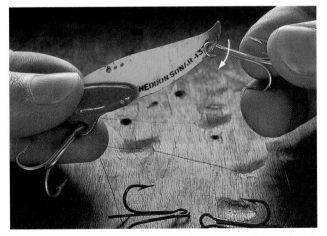

REPLACE a bent or rusty hook with a new split-eye hook by placing the free end of the eye into the attachment hole, then twisting the hook (arrow) to close the eye. Or substitute a split-ring and a standard treble.

Fishing with Tailspins

Originally, the tailspin was designed for bass fishing in southern reservoirs. But many fishermen have found it effective in northern waters for bass, walleyes and even lake trout.

Because the spinner blade on the tail turns while the lure is moving forward or sinking, it provides constant flash. The blade slows the sink rate, so fish have plenty of time to strike.

You can jig a tailspin vertically alongside cover such as standing trees and bridge pilings, or along steep structure like cliffs and submerged creek banks. You can also jig it vertically while drifting with the wind or current.

Because of its aerodynamic shape, a tailspin excels for long-distance casting. Many reservoir fishermen carry an extra rod rigged with a tailspin in case a school of largemouths, white bass or stripers suddenly breaks the surface.

Fishermen use tailspins weighing from ¼ to ½ ounce for white bass and crappies; ½ to ¾ ounce for large-mouth, smallmouth and spotted bass; and ¾ to 1 ounce for stripers.

CAST a tailspin past a surface school of white bass, large-mouths or stripers. Hold your rod tip high and reel rapidly

ATTACH a tailspin by tying your line directly to the eye. No snap or swivel is needed, because the lure does not wiggle or spin.

JIG a tailspin vertically as you drift with the wind. Raise the rod just fast enough to feel the beat of the spinner blade. Keep the line tight enough so that you also feel the beat while lowering the lure. As you drift, adjust the line length to keep the lure close to bottom.

so the lure does not sink below the fish. When you no longer see fish breaking the surface, the school has probably sounded. If this happens, let the lure sink a few seconds before starting your retrieve.

WALK a tailspin down a cliff to catch largemouth and spotted bass. Cast as close to the cliff as possible and let out line until the lure bumps a ledge or rock. Then pull sharply to lift the lure, release line and lower it again.

REEL a tailspin steadily, just fast enough to keep it above bottom obstructions like logs and brush. The spinning blade provides enough lift so the lure can be retrieved slowly without plummeting to bottom.

Spoons

Spoons

The flashy, wobbling motion of a spoon imitates that of a fleeing or crippled baitfish, triggering strikes from most species of gamefish. Spoons work best for large predators like northern pike, muskies, largemouth bass, salmon and trout. Because spoons appeal mainly to the sense of sight, they work best in relatively clear waters.

The long-standing popularity of spoons results not only from their nearly universal appeal to gamefish, but also from the relative ease of using them. Anglers normally fish spoons far enough above bottom so that snags are not a problem. And a fish usually hooks itself when it grabs a spoon.

Spoons are generally made of hard metal, either steel or brass. A few are made of tough plastic. Because one side is concave, a spoon catches water when retrieved and wobbles from side to side.

How a spoon wobbles depends on its shape and thickness. A long spoon usually has a wider side-to-side action than a short spoon. A deeply concave spoon catches more water and thus wobbles more widely than a flatter spoon. Thin spoons tend to wobble more than thick ones.

But thick spoons have some advantages. The extra weight makes them cast better, sink faster and run deeper than thin spoons.

Most spoons have a polished metal surface on at least one side. Sunlight reflecting off this surface makes the spoon visible for a long distance, especially in clear water. Some spoons have a hammered surface that scatters light in all directions, much the way the scales of a baitfish scatter light. High-quality spoons sometimes have a plated surface that reflects more light than the duller surface of cheaper spoons.

Spoons fall into three basic categories. *Standard spoons* include any non-weedless spoon heavy enough to cast. *Trolling spoons* are so thin that they are not practical for casting. Most standard and trolling spoons have a single or treble hook attached to one end with a split-ring. *Weedless spoons* usually have some type of weedguard to prevent the fixed single hook from fouling in weeds, brush or debris.

The main consideration in fishing a spoon is how fast you work it. A spoon will not wobble properly if fished too slowly or too fast. You must experiment to find the precise speed at which each spoon performs best.

Most anglers prefer light- to medium-power spinning or baitcasting tackle when fishing with spoons. Ultrasensitive rods are not necessary. Because fish tend to hook themselves on spoons, you need not be concerned about detecting strikes.

Spoons work best when fished with light monofilament. Heavy line restricts the wobble and is more visible to fish in clear water.

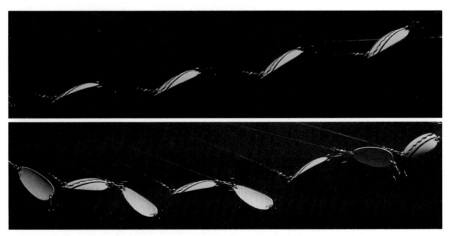

WATCH your spoon while reeling it in or trolling it alongside your boat. If the spoon slips through the water with little wobble (top), it is moving too slowly. If it wobbles enticingly from side to side (bottom), the speed is just right. If it spins, it is moving too fast.

SELECT the size of your spoon based on the size of the baitfish. It should be about as long as the baitfish's body, excluding its tail.

Standard Spoons

Standard spoons come in a confusing array of sizes, shapes and thicknesses. You can greatly improve your fishing success by learning which spoons work best for the fish you pursue and the situations you typically encounter.

The major concern in choosing standard spoons is thickness. Some manufacturers make the same design in thick, medium and thin models.

Thick spoons wobble best when retrieved rapidly. They can be cast long distances, even in a strong wind. These qualities make them ideal for exploratory fishing. When you are not sure where to find the fish, thick spoons enable you to search out a large area quickly.

A thick spoon sinks rapidly and holds its depth when retrieved. For these reasons, it is a good choice for fishing in deep water or fast current.

Thin spoons wobble attractively at slow speeds, so they work well in cold water or whenever fish are sluggish and reluctant to strike. But you cannot cast a thin spoon nearly as far or as accurately as a thick one. Thin spoons sink slowly and tend to climb on the retrieve, so they are best suited to fishing in shallow water.

Medium-thickness spoons perform best at moderate speeds. You can cast them easily. They sink fairly fast and hold their depth reasonably well. Because they work well in a wide variety of situations, they are the most popular of all spoons.

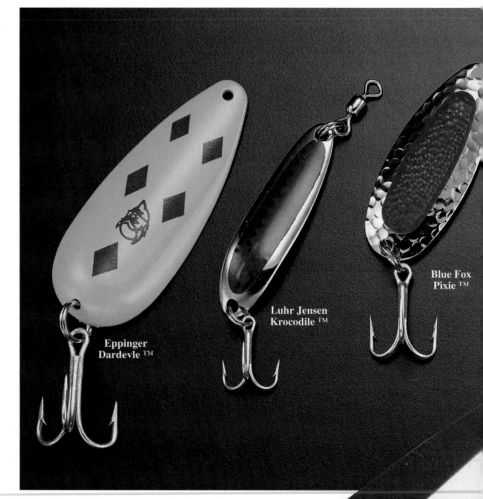

Eppinger
Dardevle ™

Luhr Jensen
Krocodile ™

Blue Fox
Pixie ™

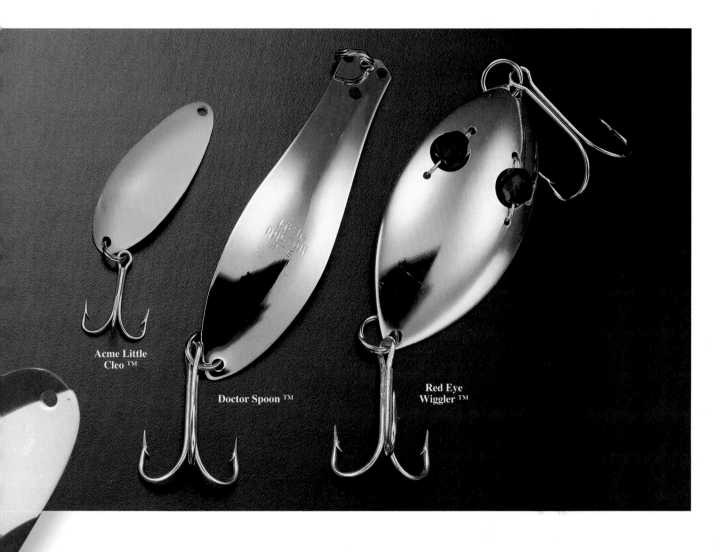

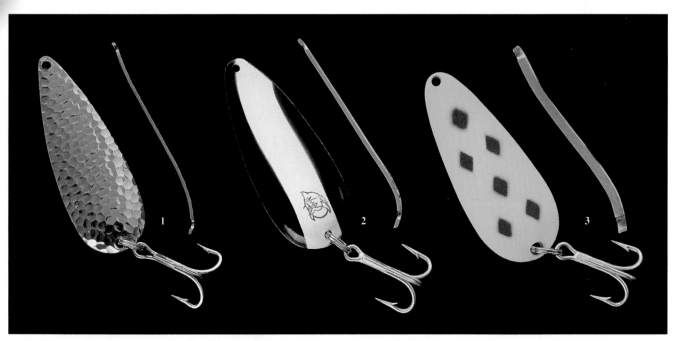

STANDARD SPOONS come in a variety of thicknesses. A (1) thin spoon 3 inches long weighs about ⅜ ounce; a (2) medium spoon of the same length, about ¾ ounce; a (3) thick spoon, approximately 1½ ounces.

Fishing with Standard Spoons

Fishermen use standard spoons for everything from long-distance casting off piers to trolling in deep water to stationary fluttering in current. This versatility, along with the simplicity of using these lures, accounts for their widespread popularity.

Although standard spoons are easy to use, many anglers make mistakes that cost them fish. Common errors include tying the line directly to the attachment hole, failing to use a swivel and retrieving at the wrong speed or depth.

If the spoon does not come with an attachment ring or rounded snap, you should add one. If you tie monofilament directly to the hole, the spoon will not wobble freely and the sharp edge will probably cut the line. To avoid severe line twist, always use a good swivel, preferably the ball-bearing type.

It pays to carry a selection of thick, medium and thin spoons. The most productive depth and retrieve speed may change from day to day, depending on variables like wind, cloud cover and the mood of the fish. With a selection of spoons of different thicknesses, you can alter your strategy to suit the conditions.

The techniques shown on the following pages specify thick or thin spoons. But in most instances, they will also work with medium-thickness spoons.

CLIP a snap-swivel directly to the hole or attachment ring. When attaching thin spoons, some fishermen prefer to splice a barrel swivel into the line 6 inches to 3 feet ahead of the lure. This prevents the swivel from interfering with the spoon's action.

How to Fish Thick Spoons from a Pier or Steep Shoreline (Countdown Technique)

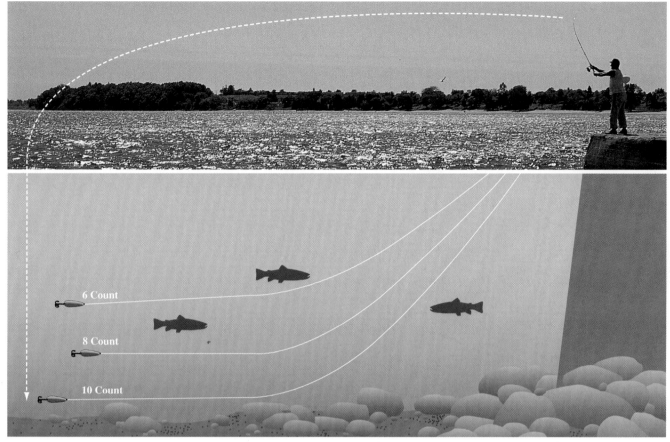

CAST a thick spoon using a 7- to 9-foot, long-handled spinning rod. A two-handed cast will give you maximum distance. To locate salmon, trout and other fish that suspend, count the spoon down to different depths after each cast. Pay out line as the spoon sinks, counting until the line goes slack. Then reel in steadily. If the spoon hits bottom on a 10-count on the first cast, count down to 8 on the second cast, 6 on the third, etc. Remember the count on each cast; if you hook a fish, count down to the same depth on the next cast.

Other Ways to Fish Thick Spoons

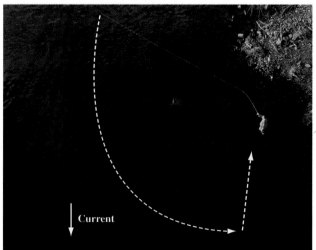

ANGLE your casts upstream in deep current. Hold your rod tip high, following the spoon as it drifts and sinks. Reel just fast enough to keep a taut line. When the spoon is directly downstream, lower your rod and retrieve with twitches to imitate a minnow struggling upstream.

RETRIEVE with sharp jerks after casting beyond a surface school of white bass, stripers or largemouths. The jerky retrieve draws strikes because the spoon acts like a shad trying to escape. Pause occasionally to let the spoon sink; the largest fish often stay deepest.

How to Fish Thin Spoons in Current

CAST across current so the spoon alights just beyond and upstream of a boulder. Work the spoon along the upstream and near sides. Next, cast beyond and below the boulder and reel quickly into the eddy. Keep the spoon wobbling there for a few seconds, then try another spot.

POSITION yourself upstream from hard-to-reach cover like an overhanging limb or undercut bank. Cast your spoon so it alights just upstream from the cover. Let the spoon drift into the spot, then hold it in place so it flutters in the current.

Other Ways to Fish Thin Spoons

FAN-CAST a thin spoon over a shallow flat. Reel steadily, keeping the spoon just off bottom. This technique works well for trout and salmon near stream mouths, for lake trout along rocky shorelines after ice-out and for northern pike in mud-bottomed bays in early spring.

RETRIEVE a thin spoon just above submerged vegetation. If you feel the spoon touching the weed tips, pull sharply to free it and to make it run shallower. Largemouths or northern pike lurking in the weeds will leave cover to grab the spoon.

Tips for Using Standard Spoons

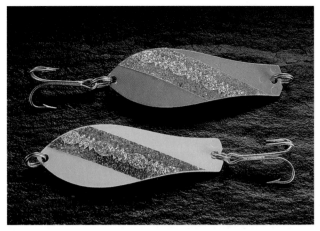

REPLACE the treble hook with a Siwash hook if you are losing too many fish. A Siwash penetrates deeper and holds better. To make your spoon run shallower, substitute a treble hook dressed with bucktail.

REVERSE a spoon by removing the hook from the split-ring and attaching it to the ring on the other end. The reversal changes the amount of wobble and may even change the depth at which the spoon runs.

SHINE tarnished spoons by using baking soda on a damp cloth. You can also use metal polish or polishing compound used for cars. If the spoon is badly tarnished or rusted, you may have to polish it with fine steel wool. A shinier spoon reflects more light, making it visible to fish at a greater distance.

ADD tape to your spoon to change its appearance. Prism tape and fluorescent tape work especially well; a thin strip often makes a big difference. Or you can color the spoon with fluorescent spray paint. Many fishermen carry small spray cans in their tackle boxes. You may have to use a white primer before applying the fluorescent paint. Waterproof marking pens can also be effective, but the color they produce is never as intense as paint. These techniques eliminate the need to carry dozens of different-colored spoons.

Trolling Spoons

Trolling spoons rank among the top lures for trophy salmon and lake trout. The slow, fluttering action often tempts big fish to strike at times when they ignore faster moving lures.

You can troll with any type of spoon, but trolling spoons were designed specifically for that purpose. Without added weight, a trolling spoon could be cast no more than a few feet and would plane to the surface when retrieved.

The fluttering, wide-swimming action of a trolling spoon results from the ultrathin design. Thicker spoons have less side-to-side action at slow speeds because the force of moving water has less effect on a heavier object of the same size and shape.

Because of the ultrathin metal, trolling spoons are less durable than other types of spoons. They often become badly bent in the process of unhooking fish. Occasionally, a fisherman retrieves the spoon and finds a sharp bend in it, the result of a fish grabbing the spoon but missing the hook. But

Luhr Jensen Coyote 4.0 ™

Luhr Jensen Diamond King ™

Blue Fox Trixee ™

Northport Nailer ™

Pro King ™

Luhr Jensen Flutter Spoon ™

TROLLING SPOONS are thinner than any other type of spoon. A typical 3-inch trolling spoon weighs about $1/8$ ounce, but some ultrathin models of the same length weigh as little as $1/16$ ounce.

TROLLING spoons often come with large Siwash hooks (left) rather than treble hooks (right). Siwash hooks are easier to remove from fish and often hook fish more solidly.

you can return most trolling spoons to their original shape simply by bending them with your fingers.

The extremely light weight of a trolling spoon makes it relatively snagless, even when trolled over a rocky bottom. Heavier spoons sink quickly when you slow down and often wedge between the rocks. Trolling spoons sink much more slowly. If they do touch bottom, they seldom wedge in place. Their resistance to snagging makes them a good choice for bottom-hugging fish like lake trout.

Fishing with Trolling Spoons

While trolling spoons have a special appeal to lake trout and salmon, they will also catch lake-dwelling rainbow and brown trout. Some fishermen use trolling spoons to search for striped bass in sprawling southern reservoirs.

You can troll these spoons without added weight when fish are near the surface. But you will need sinkers or some type of deep-trolling device when fish are deeper. Most anglers prefer downriggers so they can precisely control the depth. But many troll with wire or lead-core line, or use diving planes.

With these lures, trolling speed is critical. Some fishermen tie a pilot lure (p. 55) to their boat to monitor their speed. But a trolling-speed indicator

(p. 55) will give you a precise reading and is easier to use. Run the spoon alongside the boat to determine the proper speed, then continue at that speed once you start fishing.

An erratic trolling path generally works better than a straight one. If you troll in an S-pattern, the spoon will slow down and drop as you begin to turn, speed up and climb as you straighten out, then slow and drop again as you turn the other way. The change of speed, depth and direction often triggers a strike.

Trolling spoons wobble best when fished with light, limp line. Stiff line restricts the action more than it would with a thicker spoon.

REEL up the slack after attaching the line to the release and lowering the weight to the right depth. Continue reeling until the rod bows sharply into the set position.

WATCH your rod tip to detect a strike. When a fish grabs the lure, the release mechanism trips, slackening the line momentarily and causing the rod to snap straight.

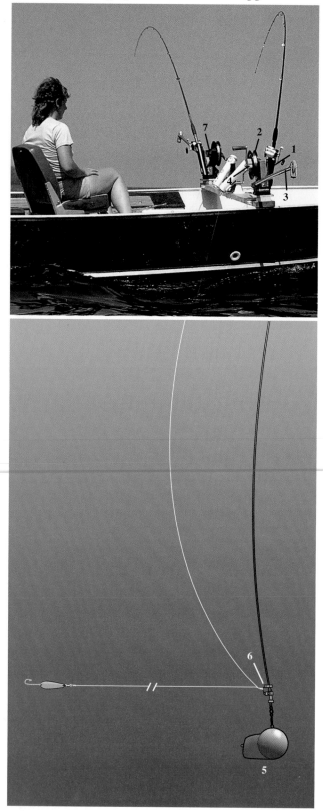

DOWNRIGGERS have a (1) rod holder, (2) large reel filled with light cable, (3) 2- to 4-foot arm to hold the cable away from the boat, (4) brake to stop the (5) 8- to 12-pound weight at the right depth, (6) line release. A (7) counter (downrigger on opposite side) registers the depth.

SET the hook after reeling up the slack line. Another angler should quickly reel up the downrigger weight to prevent the fish from tangling around the cable.

Wire-lining with Trolling Spoons

WIRE-LINING with trolling spoons works well for deepwater fish like lake trout. Wire has little water resistance and does not stretch, so you can easily reach bottom and feel strikes. To tie a wire-line rig (inset), attach a 5-foot leader of 10-pound mono to one eye of a three-way swivel. Tie a 10- to 16-ounce lead ball to another eye with 2 feet of 15-pound mono. Attach 20- to 30-pound wire line to the third eye with a haywire twist (p. 14).

How to Bend a Trolling Spoon to Improve Its Action

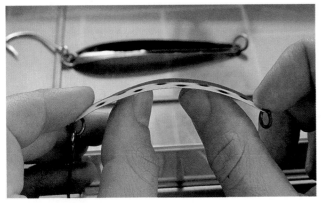

BEND a spoon by putting your thumbs together at its center, then sliding them outward while exerting pressure. The bend should be as smooth as possible. Be careful not to kink the spoon.

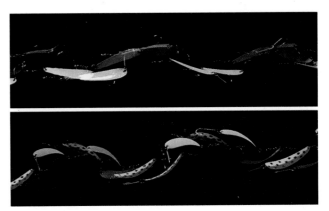

ACTION of a normal spoon (top) differs greatly from that of a bent spoon (bottom). The bent spoon catches more water, causing it to veer more sharply to the side and creating a wider wobble.

103

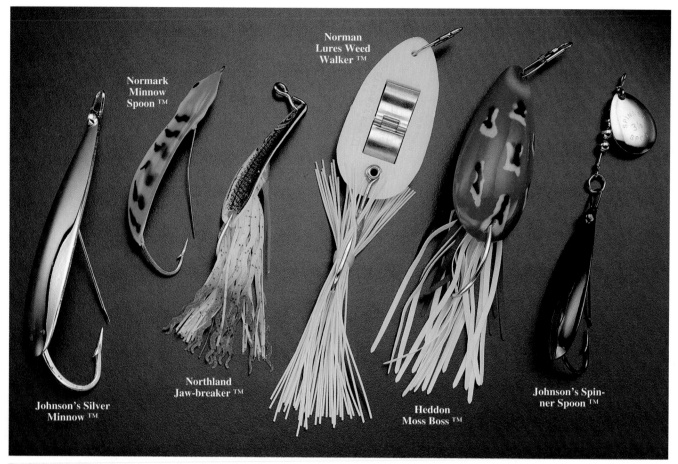

Normark
Minnow
Spoon ™

Norman
Lures Weed
Walker ™

Johnson's Silver
Minnow ™

Northland
Jaw-breaker ™

Heddon
Moss Boss ™

Johnson's Spin-
ner Spoon ™

BASIC TYPES include conventional weedless spoons, which resemble standard spoons; spinner-spoons, with some type of spinner or propeller for extra lift; spoons with an upturned lip; and plastic spoons, with a wide, lightweight body. Most weedless spoons have a rigid single hook and a metal, plastic or bristle weedguard.

Weedless Spoons

A weedless spoon can snake through weeds, brush, timber or other obstructions sure to foul most other types of lures.

Conventional weedless spoons sink rapidly, so they are a good choice for retrieving through submerged vegetation. They wobble best at moderate speed.

Spinner-spoons work better than other types when fish have difficulty seeing the lure because of the dense cover. Because the spinner or propeller provides lift, these spoons can be retrieved slowly without sinking. And fish like bass and northern pike quickly zero in on the surface commotion.

Spoons with upturned lips and plastic spoons slide across the surface more easily than other weedless spoons, so they are the best choice for fishing over thick surface vegetation. These spoons should be retrieved slowly. However, some spoons with upturned lips sink

How to Fine-tune a Weedless Spoon

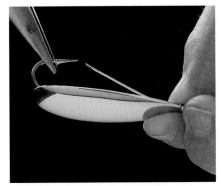

BEND the hook point outward slightly with pliers. By opening the gap, you improve your hooking percentage.

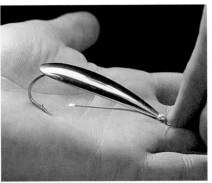

TEST the hook by pulling it across your palm. If the point catches, the gap is bent open wide enough.

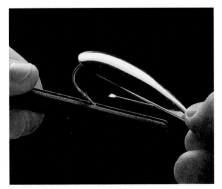

SHARPEN the hook on a grooved stone. Sharpness is vital, since the big single hook can be difficult to set.

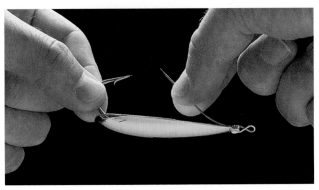

BEND the weedguard out to decrease snagging. Allow a half inch of space between the guard and hook point.

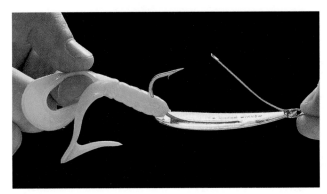

ATTACH a trailer. Align the tail with the plane of the spoon body to add lift to the lure.

Weedless Spoon Trailers

TRAILERS for weedless spoons include: (1) Pork Frog, (2) grub tail, (3) silicone skirt, (4) plastic worm, (5) plastic frog.

rapidly. They can be fished much deeper and should be retrieved at moderate speed.

Generally, weedless spoons are used with a plastic or pork-rind trailer. The trailer adds action, slows the sink rate and helps prevent the lure from spinning.

Weedless spoons have one major drawback. The weedguard and the large, thick hook make hooking fish more difficult than with other types of spoons. To improve your chances, carry a hook file and keep your hooks sharp.

Setting the hook is easiest with a stiff rod and strong line. To prevent your line from fraying on weed stems, use abrasion-resistant mono, usually 15- to 20-pound test.

Fishing with Weedless Spoons

A weedless spoon rigged with a flexible trailer has an alluring action as it slithers through the vegetation. The lures excel for largemouth bass, northern pike and pickerel in dense cover.

Because fish often have trouble locating a spoon in heavy cover, a steady retrieve generally works best, especially in unbroken expanses of weeds. An erratic retrieve will compound the problem.

Often fish will swirl or splash in an attempt to grab a weedless spoon. They frequently miss it on the first try, so you should not set the hook until you feel the strike. If you do not jerk the lure away, the fish

will probably try again. When you do set the hook, jerk as hard as you can.

Most weedless spoons are heavy and have an aerodynamic shape, so it is tempting to make long casts with them. But you will hook more fish if you keep your casts short. At long distances, line stretch makes it difficult to set the hook. And long casts are seldom necessary because fish hiding in dense cover do not spook easily.

Weedless spoons can be effective in emergent weeds as well as those below the surface. But fishing in emergent weeds can be difficult because your line may catch on the protruding stems as it settles to the water. When you try to retrieve, the spoon comes to the surface. To avoid this problem, look for alleys in the weeds and make low, flat casts. If your line still catches on the stems, shake your rod briskly to jiggle the line free.

SKIM a weedless spoon over dense surface vegetation by holding your rod tip high while reeling. Any type of weedless spoon will work, but plastic spoons or spoons with an upturned lip are easiest to keep on the surface.

RETRIEVE a conventional weedless spoon steadily through emergent weeds like bulrushes. The spoon will seldom hang up if you cast into the wind. With the stems bent toward you, the spoon can swim through more easily.

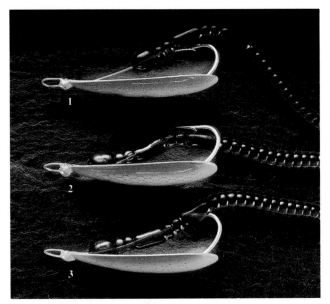

MAKE a spoon more weedless by (1) pushing a plastic worm onto the weedguard. (2) Bend the hook slightly outward so that it will penetrate the worm. Then (3) push the hook point almost through the worm.

ADD a weedless trailer hook if you are having trouble hooking fish. Push a plastic tab over the hook point, thread on the trailer, then push on another tab to hold the trailer in place.

Flies

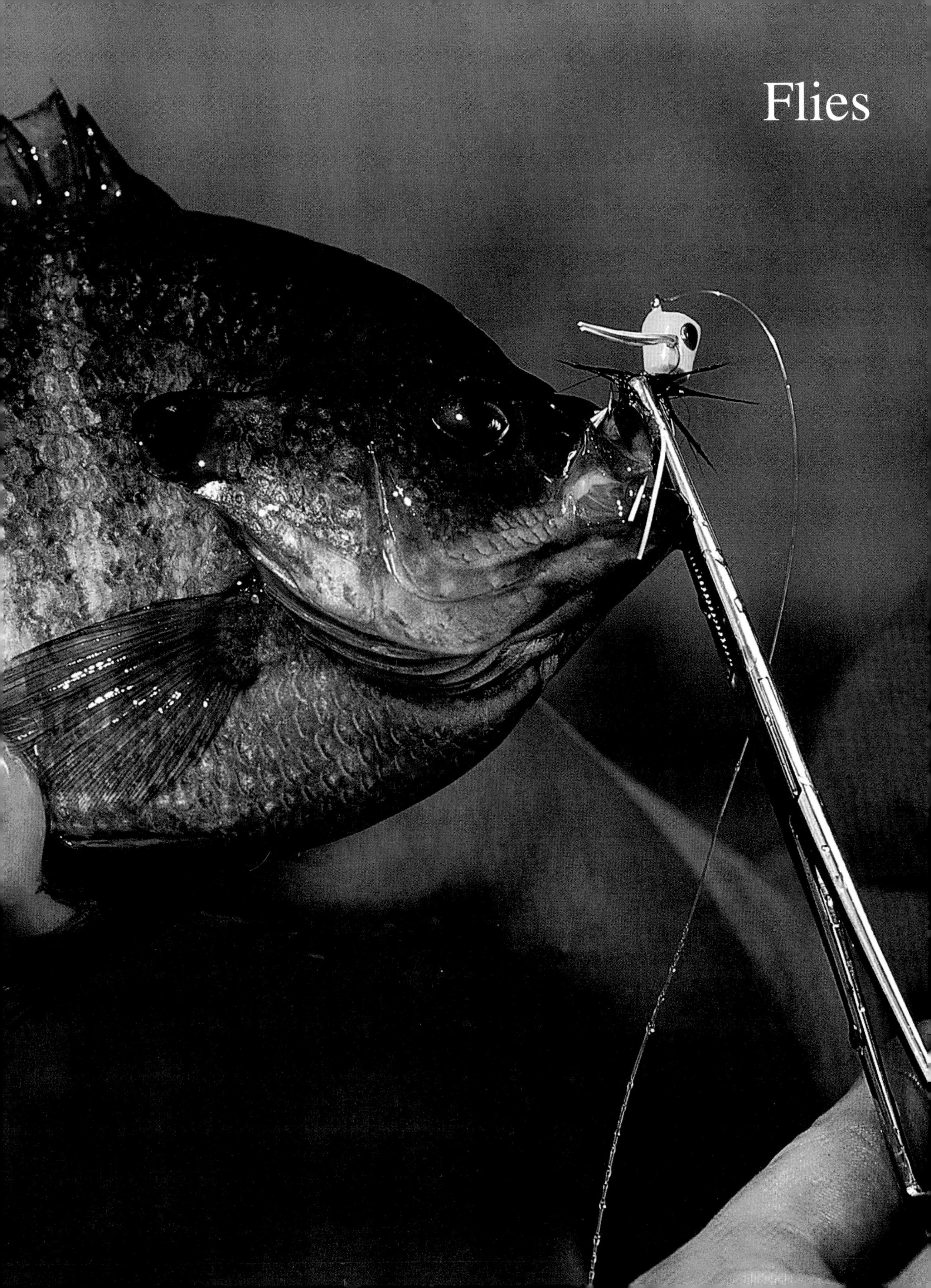

Flies

Most traditional fly patterns are *imitators,* simulating natural foods eaten by gamefish. Practically all freshwater fish rely heavily on aquatic insects at some time in their life, explaining why so many flies used in fresh water are insect imitations. The diet of most adult fish, however, leans heavily toward crustaceans and baitfish, so a lot of flies mimic these food types.

Some imitators are painstakingly realistic, with antennae, jointed legs and other body parts that closely match those of the natural bait in every respect. But that degree of imitation is seldom necessary to fool a fish; in most cases, an *impressionistic fly,* one with the general look of the natural, will do the job equally well. When choosing an imitator, consider:

SIZE. Your fly should closely match the size of the natural. An imitation that is too large, even when presented well, is likely to spook the fish.

COLOR. You can't go wrong with a fly that's similar in hue to the natural. If you can't match the color, select a fly similar in shade. If the fish are taking a light-colored mayfly, for instance, don't use a dark-colored imitation.

SHAPE. A fly with the general profile of the natural may be all it takes to convince the fish to bite. When the fish are selective, however, pay closer attention to tail length, wing size and body shape.

ACTION. The overall look of a fly is normally more important than its action. But there are times when action will trigger strikes. A fly with a marabou body, for example, may present a closer imitation of an undulating leech than does a fly with a hair body.

TEXTURE. Texture does not entice a fish to take a fly, but it may affect how long the fish holds on to the fly. A spun deer hair bug, for instance, feels more like real food than a hard-bodied bug, so a fish may mouth it for an instant longer before rejecting it, giving you more time to set the hook.

Often, you'll see insects hatching sporadically, but you won't be able to spot a predominant hatch. This is the time to try *searching patterns,* flies that represent a broad spectrum of insect life, rather than a specific insect form.

Some flies, called *attractors,* bear no resemblance to any kind of natural food. They rely on bright colors, flashy materials or sound to arouse a fish's curiosity or trigger a defensive strike.

Types of Fly Patterns

IMITATORS include Pink Scud (top) and Damselfly Nymph (bottom).

SEARCHING PATTERNS include Adams dry fly (right) and Pheasant Tail Nymph (far right).

ATTRACTORS include Royal Coachman dry fly (top) and Parmachene Belle wet fly (bottom).

Dry Flies

When fluttering insects fill the air and rising fish dimple the water, it's time to tie on a dry fly. Designed to be fished on the surface, dry flies imitate the adult forms of aquatic insects such as mayflies, stoneflies, caddisflies and midges.

Used primarily for trout, dry flies will also take Atlantic salmon, bass and panfish.

When trout gorge themselves on adult insects that are hatching, they can be quite selective, explaining why tiers have created so many dry-fly patterns.

Dry flies are fished on the surface of the water, whether it is a stream or body of still water. In almost all cases the fly is fished so that there is no drag on the fly. Drag is movement of the fly that occurs when it is pulled in a direction that is not consistent with a stream's current. Or in the case of still water, the fly isn't lying still.

Tips for Fishing Dry Flies

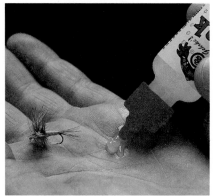

TREAT your dry fly with a fly floatant to keep it resting on the water's surface. Be sure that your fly is dry before applying the paste to the fly.

LOOK through binoculars to spot insects floating on the surface of the water. In many cases, you'll be able to identify insects at a substantial distance.

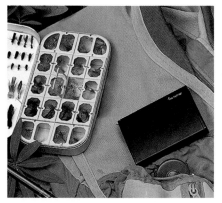

STORE dry flies in a fly box that has compartments. The compartments, as long as they are not overfilled, allow the flies to be stored without crushing the hackles.

Types of Dry-fly Patterns

Red Quill

UPRIGHT WING – The most common type of dry fly, this style has wings resembling those of a live mayfly. The wings are usually made from feathers or hair.

DOWN WING – The wings are folded back tentlike over the body of the fly to imitate a caddis or stonefly. The wings, commonly made of hair, may also be made of feathers or thin plastic film.

Hemingway Caddis

Trico Spinner

Olive Thorax

Blue-wing Olive Parachute

SPENT WING – This type imitates a dead mayfly, which floats on the water with spread wings. Most patterns have wings of feathers or poly yarn.

THORAX – The wing is tied in near the center of the hook, with dubbing on each end, to create a realistic underwater image of a mayfly.

PARACHUTE – These flies have a single upright wing, made of hair or poly yarn, that forms a base around which the hackle is wrapped horizontally.

Brown Bivisible

Brown No-hackle

Brown Variant

BIVISIBLE – A wingless pattern with dry-fly hackle wrapped palmer-style along the length of the hook shank to form the body.

NO-HACKLE – Made with quill-segment wings, these patterns float low in the surface film to imitate an emerging adult.

VARIANT – Tied with oversized hackle and usually no wings, variants imitate spiders and water skaters.

113

Nymphs

The term "nymph" refers to imitations of the larval, pupal and nymphal stages of aquatic insects. Some, called *emergers*, simulate an insect just prior to hatching. While adult insects are available to fish for only brief periods, these immature forms are present throughout the year and make up a much higher proportion of the diet.

Some nymphs are intended to simulate crustaceans, such as scuds, shrimp and crayfish.

Nymphs are effective not only for trout, but also for panfish and bass. They can be classified according to the type of immature aquatic insect they imitate.

Most of the time nymphs are fished near the bottom of the stream or lake. They are weighted or extra weight is added to the leader to get the fly to the bottom. Sink-tip or full sinking lines will also carry the nymph to the bottom.

Tips for Fishing Nymphs

PICK UP rocks and check them for clinging insects, such as caddisfly larvae and stonefly nymphs. Use a fly that is the approximate size, shape and color of the natural.

USE a strike indicator to detect light strikes when fishing with nymphs. Indicators include (1) corkie, (2) synthetic yarn, (3) float putty and (4) twist-on.

CAST nymphs in streams up and across current. Allow the nymph to drift, drag-free, downstream along the bottom. In still water, slowly work the nymph along the bottom.

Nymph Patterns

Dark Hendrickson Nymph

Giant Black Stonefly Nymph

MAYFLY NYMPH imitations have a wing case on the back, feathers or picked-out dubbing on the sides to represent the legs, and a feather or hair tail designed to mimic the two- or three-filament tail of the natural.

STONEFLY NYMPH imitations often have antennae and two-filament tails made of goose biots or other stiff feathers. The wing case usually has two or three segments.

Peeking Caddis

Marabou Midge Larva

Brassie

CASED CADDIS LARVA imitations have legs of dark material, such as peacock herl, to imitate the natural. The body is made of yarn or dubbing, with no tail.

MIDGE LARVA AND PUPA imitations are tied on very small hooks to imitate the naturals. Larva imitations are tied using marabou or floss. Pupa imitations have bodies tied of wire or floss. And a bulge, which imitates the developing legs and wings, is made of peacock herl, deer hair or other material.

Goplin Emerger

Olive Scud

EMERGERS are designed to imitate nymphs that are almost ready to hatch. The wing cases, often made of hackle-feather loops, poly yarn or a ball of dubbing, trap enough air to make the fly float in the surface film with most of the body submerged. Some patterns include a small foam ball. Emergers are tied on light-wire hooks.

SCUD imitations, tied on short-shank hooks, have epoxy or plastic shellbacks and legs of picked-out dubbing. Some have hackle-fiber antennae or tails.

Wet Flies

Wet flies were designed centuries ago to imitate drowned insects, and they are still effective for this purpose.

Most commonly used for trout and salmon, wet flies work equally well for panfish, especially crappies and sunfish.

Some wet flies, such as palmer-hackle or soft-hackle types (opposite page) have no wings and resemble crustaceans or immature or stillborn aquatic insects. Patterns tied with tinsel and iridescent feathers have the flashy look of a minnow. These attractor patterns rely on their gaudy colors.

A typical wet fly is tied using absorbent materials such as wool or chenille to help it sink easily, and soft hackles or swept-back wings give it a life-like action.

Used in moving and still water, wet flies can be fished drag-free or moving – with action added by a stream's current or by stripping the fly. Depending on the fish's depth, use wet flies weighted or unweighted, with floating, sink-tip or sinking lines.

Tips for Fishing Wet Flies

ADD twist-on lead, moldable weight or split shot a few inches above a wet fly to get it to go deeper. If the fish are too deep for a floating line, use a sink-tip or sinking line.

FISH a wet fly along the edge of a weedbed or in a pocket to catch pan-fish. Let the fly sink, trying different depths to find fish. Strip the line slow-ly along the cover.

CAST a wet fly across current in streams. For deeper water, angle the cast slightly upstream so the fly can sink longer before the current sweeps it downstream.

Blue Dun

Undertaker

TRADITIONAL WET FLIES are usually tied with feather wings (left), but some have hair wings (right). Feather-wing patterns, with wings made of hackle tips or quill segments, commonly imitate drowned adult insects. Most hair-wing patterns imitate baitfish. Because hair is buoyant, the hooks are sometimes wrapped with wire or they have a brass bead head to sink the fly. Less realistic, but more durable, they sink faster and have more action, especially when retrieved with an erratic motion.

Partridge-and-Yellow

Red Abbey

SOFT-HACKLE flies are sparsely tied, normally with a hackle collar but no wings. They sink quickly and have good action, so they make excellent imitations of immature aquatic insects or crustaceans.

Yellow Wooly Worm

PALMER-HACKLE flies have hackle wound over the entire length of the body, but no wings. They resemble terrestrials, immature aquatic insects or crustaceans. Like soft-hackle flies, they work well with a twitching retrieve.

Gordon

SALMON FLIES rely on their bright colors to attract fish and are not intended to imitate real stream life. Some patterns, like the Gordon, are extremely intricate. Called "fully dressed," many of these artistic creations are tied for display purposes only and never see water. Fully dressed salmon flies are expensive because they are difficult to tie and often call for rare or exotic materials that can no longer be legally imported.

Streamers

As freshwater gamefish grow larger, their diet generally includes fewer insects and more baitfish. This explains why streamers, which simulate baitfish, are such effective big-fish flies.

Streamers will take practically any kind of gamefish, including trout and salmon; largemouth, smallmouth and spotted bass; white and striped bass; crappies; and northern pike, muskies and pickerel.

Like wet flies, streamers are often tied using absorbent materials to help them sink. Weight, such as lead wire, is added to help reach deeper lies of gamefish. Some streamers have realistic eyes for extra attraction and monofilament weedguards for fishing in weeds.

Streamers work equally well in still or moving water. In a stream, the current gives streamers action, but often it is necessary to add movement by stripping the fly. In still waters, you must strip the fly to give it action. At times, fish prefer a slow retrieve, while at other times, you must strip the line as fast as you can to draw strikes from the fish.

Tips for Fishing Streamers

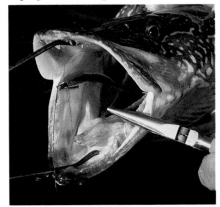

USE a wire leader when using streamers for fish with sharp teeth. Fish such as northern pike, muskies and pickerel will easily bite through a monofilament tippet.

FISH a tandem streamer rig for schooling fish such as white bass. At times, after a fish takes one fly, others will follow and try to steal it, often taking the second fly.

STRIP a streamer in still or slow-moving water with the rod tip only inches above the surface. This will minimize slack line and increase your hooking percentage.

Types of Streamers

Light Spruce

HACKLE-WING STREAMERS have a wing made of long, relatively stiff hackle feathers. These flies sink readily, so they can be fished fairly deep, even with a floating line. They work well in both moving and still water.

Muddler Minnow   **Royal Coachman Bucktail**

MUDDLERS have large heads of clipped deer hair and wings of turkey quill segments, marabou or hackle feathers. Highly versatile, they work in still or moving water. Most muddlers float, or sink very slowly. But some are wound with lead wire so they can be fished on bottom.

BUCKTAIL STREAMERS have a wing made of bucktail, calf tail or other hair. They sink more slowly than hackle-wings, but can be fished deep with a sinking or sink-tip line. Like hackle-wings, bucktails work well in moving and still water.

MATUKA STREAMERS have a hackle-feather wing secured the entire length of the body with thread or tinsel. This way, the wing never becomes fouled in the hook bend, as it may on a hackle-wing. The wing forms an upright keel, giving the fly good stability in fast water.

Black Matuka

MARABOU STREAMERS have a fluffy marabou wing that assumes the shape of a baitfish when the fly is wet. A marabou streamer sinks more slowly than a hackle-wing. When twitched, the fly has a pulsating action, so it works well in either still or moving water.

Janssen Black Marabou

Terrestrials

Whether or not a hatch is on, trout won't hesitate to grab an ant, beetle or other terrestrial insect. Terrestrials work equally well for bass and panfish, and they're just as effective in still water as in streams.

Terrestrial imitations are a good choice in summer, when the wind blows large numbers of land insects into the water. But these flies are an option any time the naturals are available.

Tied with buoyant materials so they float on the surface, terrestrials can be twitched to mimic the struggle of a live insect.

Most terrestrial imitations are fished in the surface film or on the surface of the water. A few are fished below the surface. Unlike dry flies, action can be added to the fly as it rests on the surface because terrestrials often struggle when they land in the water. These flies are most productive when fished near grassy banks or brush, locations where insects are blown into the water by the wind.

Tips for Fishing Terrestrials

OVERPOWER the forward stroke of the cast, transferring the energy through the fly line and straightened leader and onto the fly. Stop the cast with the rod tip pointed at the exact spot you want the fly to land. Don't aim above the target, as you would when casting other dry flies, because the fly will not plop into the water.

CAST terrestrial imitations along overhanging brush or in areas where grassy banks meet the water's edge, locations where fish commonly find terrestrial insects.

Types of Terrestrials

GRASS HOPPER AND CRICKET imitations often have feather wings and jointed legs. Tied on long-shank hooks, in sizes 6 to 14, they work best in late summer.

Dave's Cricket

ANT imitations have a segmented body and are tied on standard-length hooks, usually in sizes 14 to 20. These flies are effective throughout the season.

Black Fur Ant

Caterpillar

Black Beetle

BEETLE imitations can be year-round producers. Most have a deer-hair or foam shellback and are tied on standard-length hooks, usually in sizes 12 to 18.

OTHER terrestrial insect imitations include caterpillars (above), inchworms (right) and practically every other conceivable type, from jassids to walkingsticks.

Inchworm

Bugs & Specialty Flies

Few other lures work as well when fish are feeding on surface foods like large insects, frogs or mice.

But bugs can be effective even if you don't see fish feeding on the surface. They work particularly well for many warm-water species during the spawning period and are a good option whenever fish are in the shallows.

These flies range in size from the inch-long sponge bugs used for panfish to the 10-inch divers used for

Asmashing surface strike ranks as one of the most exciting moments in fishing. But excitement is not the only reason for using these topwater flies.

Types of Bugs

Bass King **Hair Popper** **Chug Bug**

POPPERS have a cupped or flattened face that produces a popping sound when the fly is twitched. They have bodies of foam, clipped deer hair, cork or balsa wood, often with hackle collars, hair or feather tails and rubber legs.

DIVERS imitate frogs or wounded minnows. They are similar to poppers, but the top of the head slopes back, causing them to dive when pulled forward. As they submerge, most divers gurgle and emit an air bubble. On the pause, they float back toward the surface.

Dahlberg's Mega Diver

SPONGE BUGS have a soft body, so fish will hold them longer than they will hard-bodied bugs. Most have rubber legs and resemble terrestrials. Used primarily for panfish, sponge bugs float low on the water or ride just beneath the surface.

Creepy Cricket

SLIDERS. Because of their bullet-shaped head, sliders cause less surface disturbance than poppers, so they work better for spooky fish. You can skitter them over fast water or slip them over dense surface cover. The streamlined shape makes them easier to cast in the wind.

Hard-bodied Slider

REALISTIC BUGS include mouse imitations (right) and frog imitations (far right). You can also find flies tied to simulate large insects and practically any other kind of food a good-size gamefish is likely to eat.

Mouserat

Whit's Wiggle-leg Frog

pike and muskies. Because of their weight and wind resistance, these large flies can be difficult to cast, so many are tied with lightweight materials, such as clipped deer hair, marabou and synthetic materials, in order to appear bulkier than they really are.

While most bugs imitate some type of real food, some attract fish mainly by the surface disturbance.

Specialty flies do not fit in any of the usual fly categories, but they work extremely well in a variety of specific fishing situations.

When smallmouth bass are gorging themselves on crayfish, for instance, a crayfish imitation works better than a streamer or any other kind of fly. Similarly, nothing can top an egg fly when rainbows are feeding heavily on the roe of spawning salmon.

Types of Specialty Flies

Clouser's Crayfish　　　　　　**Dave's Crayfish**

CRAYFISH FLIES have feathers, tufts of hair or other material tied to imitate the pincers of a crayfish. They work well for crayfish feeders like smallmouth bass, spotted bass and large trout.

Chamois Leech　　　　　**Black Leech**

LEECH FLIES have a long tail made of marabou or a strip of chamois or rabbit fur, giving the fly an undulating action similar to that of a leech. These flies appeal mainly to bass, panfish and trout.

EGG FLIES are used mainly for steelhead, salmon and trout. These simple flies are tied with fluorescent material to imitate a single egg or a cluster of eggs drifting with the current. They can also be tied with white hackle to imitate a spermed egg.

Single Egg　　　**Egg Cluster**　　　**Krystal Egg**

Index

Creative Publishing international, Inc. offers
a variety of how-to books.
For information write:

  Creative Publishing international, Inc.
   Subscriber books
  5900 Green Oak Drive
  Minnetonka, MN 55343

Books available from the publisher: *The Art of
Freshwater Fishing, The New Cleaning & Cooking
Fish, Fishing With Live Bait, Largemouth Bass,
Panfish, The Complete Guide to Hunting, Fishing
With Artificial Lures, Successful Walleye Fishing,
Smallmouth Bass, Dressing & Cooking Wild Game,
Freshwater Gamefish of North America, Trout, Fishing
Rivers & Streams, Fishing Tips & Tricks, Whitetail
Deer, Northern Pike & Muskie, The Art of Fly Tying,
America's Favorite Wild Game Recipes, Advanced Bass
Fishing, Upland Game Birds, North American Game
Animals, North American Game Birds, Advanced
Whitetail Hunting, Understanding Whitetails, Fly-
Fishing Equipment & Skills, Fishing Nymphs, Wet Flies
& Streamers, Fly-Tying Techniques & Patterns, Fishing
Dry Flies, Bowhunting Equipment & Skills, Wild Turkey,
Muzzleloading, Duck Hunting, Venison Cookery, Game
Bird Cookery, Fly Fishing for Trout in Streams, Fishing
for Catfish, Modern Methods of Ice Fishing*

Creative Publishing international is the most complete source of How-To Information for the Outdoorsman

THE COMPLETE HUNTER™ *Series*

- *White-tailed Deer*
- *Dressing & Cooking Wild Game*
- *Advanced Whitetail Hunting*
- *Bowhunting Equipment & Skills*
- *Understanding Whitetails*
- *Venison Cookery*
- *Muzzleloading*
- *Wild Turkey*
- *Duck Hunting*
- *America's Favorite Wild Game Recipes*
- *Upland Game Birds*
- *The Complete Guide to Hunting*
- *Game Bird Cookery*
- *North American Game Birds*
- *North American Game Animals*

The Freshwater Angler™ *Series*

- *Largemouth Bass*
- *The New Cleaning & Cooking Fish*
- *Fishing Tips & Tricks*
- *Trout*
- *Panfish*
- *All-Time Favorite Fish Recipes*
- *Fishing for Catfish*
- *Fishing With Artificial Lures*
- *Successful Walleye Fishing*
- *Advanced Bass Fishing*
- *The Art of Fly Tying*
- *The Art of Freshwater Fishing*
- *Fishing Rivers & Streams*
- *Northern Pike & Muskie*
- *Freshwater Gamefish of North America*
- *Fishing With Live Bait*
- *Fly Fishing for Trout in Streams*

The Complete FLY FISHERMAN™ *Series*

- *Fly-Tying Techniques & Patterns*
- *Fly-Fishing Equipment & Skills*
- *Fishing Nymphs, Wet Flies & Streamers – Subsurface Techniques for Trout in Streams*
- *Fishing Dry Flies – Surface Presentations for Trout in Streams*

FOR A LIST OF PARTICIPATING RETAILERS NEAR YOU, CALL **1-800-328-0590**